Harnessing the Storm

Harnessing the Storm

ADHD as your success catalyst

Sean M Ashley

Published by SMA Media Press. Printed in the United States of America.

ISBN: 979-8-9924987-1-4

Contents

Preface

If you have ADHD, you will understand the metaphor in this book. It describes that constant storm racing around in your head —a relentless and unpredictable force that consumes your thoughts, actions, and emotions. ADHD can feel chaotic, with your mind swept up in unyielding winds, flashes of brilliance, and overwhelming downpours of emotion. Although chaotic storms have their destructive side, they can also symbolize renewal, power, and beauty. I hope that Harnessing the Storm will guide you to step into the heart of your ADHD experience, not to resist that ever-present storm, but to embrace it.

I wrote this book because I know how isolating and misunderstood ADHD can feel. It plagued my life, hedged my way to a successful career, and put incredible strain on my relationships. Whether you're navigating the challenges of work, relationships, or personal well-being, when you have ADHD, the world looks at you like you're broken or you lack or need to be "fixed." But that's not the full story. ADHD is a constant storm in your mind; however, it's also a reservoir of energy, creativity, resilience, and power. The key is learning how to channel that energy, turning the elements of the storm into tools of empowerment, growth, and success.

In these pages, we'll embark on a journey to explore the elements of the ADHD storm—the wind, the rain, the thunder, the lightning, the fog, and the whirlwinds. Each element represents a core aspect of ADHD, from distractibility to emotional intensity, from impulsivity to hyper-focus. But we don't stop there. For every challenge, there is a counterbalance or solution for navigating the storm, transforming the chaos into strategic tools. These mindsets allow you to harness the storm's power instead of being consumed by it. Together, these tools will form your shelter, a haven where you can find calm and security amidst chaos, clarity instead of confusion, and strength in your vulnerabilities.

Importantly, it's not about perfection. It's about progress. It's about creating a life where ADHD is not a limitation or barrier at every corner. But a unique and integral part of who you are. On your journey through these pages, I'll share practical strategies, empowering insights, and real-world tools to help you navigate your journey. But more importantly, you need to know you are not alone in your storm. There is hope, support, and a way forward.

Along the way, we'll look at the individual elements of the storm and teach you new strategies. "And YES" with ADHD, it can be challenging. Sticking to a plan can feel daunting. I've created additional resources to support you beyond these pages. From a companion workbook, a self-awareness journal, a newsletter packed with encouragement and tips, and in the future, coaching programs to give you that extra help to build and maintain your shelter. These tools are designed to help you implement them because I know just how hard it can be, which is why I wrote this book the way that I did. I broke it into chunks to cater to the unique way the ADHD mind processes information. Additionally, our Newsletters and blog are available right now at **www.itswhatmattersmost.com**, to give you the courage to navigate the storm.

Harnessing the Storm is more than a guide—it's an invitation to see your ADHD in a new light. By embracing the storm, building your shelter, and leaning into your strengths, you'll discover that ADHD isn't something to conquer; it's something to understand, harness, and use. You are blessed and the Lord would never give you a challenge without a way to overcome it. Together, let's navigate the Tempest and transform this storm into a source of strength, creativity, and empowerment.

Welcome to your journey.

Let's harness the storm together.

"The storm is not something to fear; it is a force to understand, to navigate, and to harness. Within its chaos lies the energy to transform, and within you lies the strength to rise."

CHAPTER 1

Introduction: The Nature of ADHD

ADHD, or Attention-Deficit/Hyperactivity Disorder, is misunderstood by the neurotypical world, and its complexity leads to misleading stereotypes. Society portrays ADHD as something a child would suffer from. The out-of-control and hyperactive kid. You are labeled as lacking discipline, lazy, irresponsible, or a chronic procrastinator. Often viewed as someone who is "less than," These views fail to acknowledge the profound depth of what it means to live with ADHD. The neurotypical society doesn't understand the challenges, the unique strengths, and the reality of navigating a condition that touches every corner of your life.

ADHD is not merely an inability to focus or sit still. It is a neurological difference—a unique way of thinking, feeling, and experiencing the world. For us who live with it, ADHD affects how you process information, regulate emotions, form relationships, and approach work and responsibilities. Those who are neurodivergent and pegged as "scatter-brained" or "impulsive" live with a constant storm in their minds. it's a condition that influences both the internal landscape of the mind and the external interactions with the world. ADHD is an internal storm—a whirlwind of thoughts, emotions, and energy that can be as unpredictable as it is powerful.

Life in the Storm

Living with ADHD feels like being in a constant storm. It's not just when you need to get something done or stay focused; it's there 24/7. Like standing in the center of a tempest, where gusts of wind tug at your attention, pulling you from one thing to another. The rain pours down, soaking you to the bone, and it keeps you awake at night, intensifying everything. It reflects the intense emotions that often accompany ADHD, soaking through even the most carefully constructed plans. Above it all, flashes of lightning streak across the sky, like the bursts of creativity, insight, and brilliance that define the ADHD mind.

We can agree that the storm can feel overwhelming. It can leave you drenched in frustration when tasks go unfinished, buffeted by self-doubt when impulsivity leads to mistakes, and exhausted from the effort it takes to navigate a world built for different brains. It's a relentless battle against the elements, an unending struggle to stay upright amidst the chaos.

But the storm isn't just a source of challenge; it's also a wellspring of power. Those same gusts of wind that scatter your thoughts can, with the right tools, be harnessed into creativity and productivity. The emotional rain that seems so unrelenting also fosters growth, nurturing deep emotional connections and empathy. And lightning, though fleeting, can illuminate new paths, spark extraordinary ideas, and catapult you to success beyond your wildest expectations.

You Are A Force of Nature

Like a storm, ADHD is a force of nature that cannot be ignored or wished away. Just as it's possible to harness the power of wind, rain, and lightning, you can harness the storm within. By learning to work with ADHD, you can channel your inner storm. Here's the key: don't fight the storm or try to suppress it; instead, learn to understand its patterns, anticipate its shifts, and use its energy to fuel growth and transformation.

It's going to require a major shift in thinking. Society has trained us to see ADHD as a deficit, a disorder to be fixed or managed. But what if we saw it differently? What if, instead of focusing solely on its challenges, we find its potential? What if we could turn the storm into a source of strength, using its power to drive us forward rather than hold us back? That's just the thing: it is possible, and you can finally turn the tides in your favor.

Your Roadmap to Harnessing the Storm Within.

Daunting as it may seem, understanding ADHD as a storm provides a new way to navigate your unique way of processing information. It's not about erasing the storm or wishing for sunny skies every day; it's about thriving within the storm, navigating its challenges with skill and resilience. This is a roadmap for that journey, combining practical tools, scientific insights, and empowering metaphors to help you understand your unique mind.

The Journey ahead will guide you through the process of building your toolkit, your windmill, your umbrella, and your lightning rod. You'll learn how to turn distraction into focus, how to manage emotional downpours with grace, and how to channel bursts of energy into sustained progress. As you move forward, you'll realize that the storm isn't meant to be feared but rather embraced. It's your resource for movement, change, and possibility, reminding you that your mind is dynamic, vibrant, and certainly full of potential.

When people hear the term ADHD, they default to the societal definition of a hyperactive child bouncing off walls or a scatterbrained adult who can't sit still. These stereotypes are not only inaccurate but harmful, condemning a complex condition to a problem that needs to be fixed. ADHD is far more than an excess of energy or a lack of attention—it is a diverse neurological profile that includes strengths, challenges, and unique ways of experiencing the world. In other words, ADHD doesn't mean you are broken, it simply means your brain processes information differently.

Let's look at it this way: ADHD is like the wind in a storm. Left unchecked, this wind can scatter thoughts, disrupt plans, and create chaos. It is that constant push and pull of distraction, pulling focus from one thing to another in rapid succession. But the wind, when harnessed by a windmill, becomes a source of power. In the same way, understanding and managing ADHD can turn its unpredictable energy into a driving force for achievement and creativity.

Let me guide you through the process of identifying these "winds" in your life—the distractions, the impulsivity, the racing thoughts—and teach you to build your windmill, a structure that transforms chaos into productivity and focus. The first order of business is to have an understanding of what's going on in that mind of yours.

Understanding the Science of ADHD

Let's first take a deeper look into the science of ADHD. At its core, ADHD is a neurological condition. It involves differences in how the brain processes dopamine. It's the neurotransmitter that is associated with motivation and reward. The ADHD brain has a hard time producing enough dopamine giving you lower levels. Low levels of dopamine can create challenges with executive functions, the skills that are required for planning, organization, impulse control, and emotional regulation. It is the essence of neurological mechanisms that influence how individuals think, feel, and behave. It's a condition shaped by brain structure, neurochemistry, and connectivity, all of which contribute to the challenges and strengths of the ADHD mind. To better understand this complex condition, we can look to the growing body of scientific research, like the work of Dr. Stephen Faraone.

One of Dr. Faraone's well-documented findings in ADHD research is the role of dopamine, a neurotransmitter central to the brain's reward system. Dopamine helps regulate motivation, pleasure, and focus, but in individuals with ADHD, this system operates differently. According to research by Dr. Faraone, ADHD is linked to reduced dopamine signaling, which can manifest as difficulty sustaining attention, procrastination, and a tendency to seek out high-stimulation activities that provide bursts of dopamine. This is like the storm's lightning, bursts of intense energy or focus that strike unpredictably. For those with ADHD, the brain craves stimulation but struggles to maintain it consistently, leading to a cycle of hyper-focus and distraction. Strategies to regulate dopamine, such as medication, exercise, or structured routines, act as a "lightning rod," channeling this energy into productive outcomes (ref ADHD Evidence Project)

ADHD is also characterized by executive dysfunction, which involves impaired regulation of core mental skills like planning, organization, and impulse control. These skills are managed by the prefrontal cortex, often referred to as the brain's "control tower." Functional MRI studies show that this area of the brain is less active in individuals with ADHD, contributing to difficulties in managing daily tasks and regulating emotions.

A meta-analysis led by Dr. Faraone and others highlighted that both stimulant and non-stimulant ADHD medications can improve executive function, particularly working memory and cognitive flexibility. However, non-pharmacological approaches such as mindfulness and physical activity have also shown promise in supporting executive function.

Understanding the science of ADHD is like learning to read the weather. It equips you with the tools to anticipate storms, interpret their patterns, and respond with strategies that turn fleeting bursts of lightning into lasting sources of light.

ADHD is not only a cognitive condition but an emotional one. With ADHD, you can experience intense emotions, shifting quickly from joy to frustration, excitement to overwhelm. These emotions, like the rain in a storm, can feel relentless and unmanageable, soaking through every aspect of your life.

ADHD impacts emotional regulation, creating challenges that feel as overwhelming as the storm's rain. Studies indicate that irregular connectivity between the prefrontal cortex and the limbic system (responsible for emotion) contributes to intense, rapidly shifting emotions. For example, feelings of frustration may escalate quickly into anger, or moments of excitement might lead to impulsive decision-making (ref. <u>ADHD Evidence Project</u>)

Understanding this emotional turbulence helps explain why you often experience heightened reactions to stress or criticism. Strategies like therapy, mindfulness practices, and medication serve as an "umbrella," offering protection and resilience against emotional downpours.

Rain is not inherently negative; it nourishes growth and renewal. But without an umbrella, it leaves you drenched and cold. Similarly, the emotional challenges of ADHD can be managed with the right tools and strategies. Your umbrella might take the form of mindfulness practices, therapy, or supportive relationships that shield against emotional downpours. By learning to open your umbrella, you can navigate your emotions without being consumed by them.

Another key aspect of ADHD is the brain's connectivity. Research has shown irregular communication between brain regions, particularly within the default mode network (DMN), which governs mind-wandering. This overactivity in the DMN can make it challenging to stay present or focused, further compounding difficulties with attention or task completion (ref. ADHD Evidence Project)

These connectivity issues illustrate why the ADHD brain often feels like a whirlwind, pulling you in multiple directions at once. Tools like timers, external reminders, and structured environments help ground this whirlwind, enabling individuals to regain clarity and focus.

The neurological underpinnings of ADHD reveal a mind that operates differently, not deficiently. As Dr. Faraone emphasizes, ADHD is not just a list of challenges; it is a complex interplay of strengths and vulnerabilities. While the storm of ADHD can feel overwhelming, understanding its foundation provides the tools to navigate it effectively.

From channeling dopamine with structured routines to using therapy as emotional support. Each strategy is a tool to tame the storm's energy without diminishing its brilliance. By embracing these tools, individuals with ADHD can transform fleeting moments of insight and creativity into enduring sources of achievement and fulfillment.

Now that we've explored ADHD as a storm, the force of nature is both chaotic and creative. You may find that this metaphor resonates deeply because the experience of living with ADHD often feels like standing in the eye of a perpetual storm. Thoughts whirl like gusts of wind, emotions cascade like relentless rain, and ideas strike unpredictably like bolts of lightning. It's not just a momentary storm—it's a daily reality, an internal weather system that rarely quiets.

This constant storm can feel overwhelming because there is never a moment of true calm. The wind of racing thoughts pulls you in countless directions at once, scattering your focus and leaving you unsure where to begin. The rain of emotions blurs your vision, making it hard to see the path ahead or even believe you can weather the downpour. And the lightning, though brilliant and full of potential, can feel startling and fleeting, illuminating possibilities one moment only to plunge you into darkness the next.

But the storm is not just chaos; it is also power. Within every gust of wind, every drop of rain, and every bolt of lightning lies the potential for transformation. The same storm that feels unmanageable can also be a source of creativity, resilience, and strength. That is if you learn how to harness it.

Just as a sailor reads the skies to navigate the sea in darkness. Individuals with ADHD can learn to navigate their internal storms with skill and confidence. Remember, it doesn't mean you tame the storm or make it disappear; rather, it involves working with it, understanding its patterns, and using its energy to propel you forward. Each element of the storm has a counterpart a hidden solution, a tool, a strategy that transforms struggle into strength. The windmill harnesses the wind, the umbrella shields from the rain, and the lightning rod channels the storm's energy into brilliance.

Your journey ahead is about discovering your tools and learning how to use them. It's about recognizing that the storm is not your enemy; it's a part of who you are. By embracing your storm (which is unique to you), you can find ways to not only survive but thrive. The challenges of ADHD may not vanish, but your perspective, strategies, and resilience will transform how you navigate them.

As we explore the storm of ADHD, remember this: every storm eventually passes, and even the most turbulent skies contain moments of clarity and peace. Within the heart of every storm lies an opportunity for renewal, growth, and discovery. ADHD does not define you. Let me say that again "ADHD Doesn't Define You."What defines you; is your ability to face the storm, harness its power, and use it as a driving force in your life.

This is your map to navigating the storm, helping you transform its energy into something extraordinary. Together, we'll explore each element—the wind, the rain, the thunder, the lightning, and the shelter from which you navigate the storm. We'll Discover strategies and tools that will allow you to steer your course with confidence, Purpose, and Power.

Embracing the Storm

Here is your invitation to do just that: to embrace your storm, and acknowledge that ADHD is not simply a problem to solve but a part of who you are. A part that, when understood and nurtured, can become one of your greatest assets.

To embrace the storm is to accept its dual nature: its capacity for chaos and its potential to move you to creativity and take advantage of those flashes of brilliance.

In your journey ahead, we'll explore the many elements of your storm. We will examine the winds of distraction, the rain of emotional intensity, and the lightning of hyper-focus and creativity. For every challenge, I'll teach you a corresponding strength or strategy: a windmill to harness the wind, an umbrella to shield you from the rain, and a lightning rod to channel that elusive flash of brilliance, channeling its energy into a hyper-focus of useful creativity.

Your Invitation

As you embark on this journey, know that you are not alone. Millions of people navigate their storms of ADHD every day, each finding their ways to adapt, grow, and thrive. The strategies and insights in this book are not about fitting into someone else's mold but about discovering what works for you, what allows you to turn the unique challenges of ADHD into a personal source of power.

ADHD is not the absence of calm but the presence of energy. It is not a limitation but a difference. Like the storm, ADHD carries within it the seeds of renewal and transformation. This is your guide to harnessing that energy, finding your rhythm within the storm, and using it to create a life that feels meaningful, fulfilling, and authentically yours.

The journey of living with ADHD is as much about self-acceptance as it is about education. I spent years battling self-doubt, stigma, and frustration, but now, seeing ADHD as a source of strength has been transformative and liberating. By embracing an accurate, empowering understanding of ADHD, you can begin to appreciate your unique perspective and develop strategies that align with your natural strengths.

ADHD isn't a barrier to success—it's a different path. As we move through this Journey, you will find a wealth of strategies, tips, and insights designed to help you thrive in work, relationships, and personal well-being. Each step forward represents an opportunity to harness the unique power of your ADHD mind, transforming it from a storm of challenges into a catalyst for growth and achievement.

"You can't stop the wind, but you can build a windmill. ADHD isn't about resisting the storm; it's about learning how to use it."

CHAPTER 2

The Wind and the Windmill

Imagine standing in the middle of a field as a powerful wind rushes past you. It tugs at your clothing, pulls you in every direction, and scatters your belongings across the ground. Sound familiar? This is what distractibility feels like: a relentless force pulling your attention from one task to the next, leaving behind a trail of unfinished projects and growing frustration.

Understanding Distractibility

Distractibility is one of the hallmark symptoms of ADHD. It's not just about noticing a lot of things at once; it's about struggling to filter out what's unimportant from what truly matters most. With ADHD, your brain is wired for novelty, constantly scanning for stimuli that seem interesting or urgent. While this trait can lead to moments of creativity and discovery, it also means that maintaining focus on a single task can feel a bit like herding cats or battling against the wind. Here are some symptoms you may relate to:

External Distractions: People with ADHD often find their attention pulled by sights, sounds, and interruptions in their environment. A notification on their phone, a conversation in the background, or even a bird outside the window can derail their focus entirely.

Internal Distractions: Just as challenging are the internal distractions—racing thoughts, sudden ideas, or intrusive worries. These mental gusts of wind can pull focus inward, leaving individuals lost in thought rather than engaged with the task at hand.

This lack of focus can be costly and often is. When the wind of distractibility takes over, it can feel impossible to make progress. It's easy to start tasks, but they are abandoned halfway through. Important deadlines are missed as your attention shifts to less urgent (but more stimulating) activities. This scattered focus can lead to:

Overwhelm: A sense of drowning in incomplete tasks with no clear path forward.

Frustration: Feeling unable to control where your mind goes, despite wanting to stay on track.

Self-Doubt: Repeatedly losing focus can lead to negative self-talk as individuals begin to question their abilities or worth.

These challenges aren't just about productivity—they affect self-esteem, relationships, and emotional well-being. The wind of ADHD feels like a force beyond control, constantly blowing you off course.

The Windmill: As chaotic and unpredictable as the wind can be, it is also a source of power. Think of a windmill: a structure designed to harness the force of the wind, turning it into productive energy. For those of us with ADHD, the windmill represents systems and strategies that channel scattered focus into meaningful progress. You can't stop the wind, so work with it, transform it, and use its energy to create something purposeful.

Building Your Windmill: Strategies for Focus

Time-Blocking: Creating Structured Focus Time-blocking is one of the most effective tools for managing ADHD distractibility. It involves dividing your day into blocks of time, each dedicated to a specific task or activity.

Start by identifying your priorities for the day. Choose no more than three major tasks to focus on, ensuring they're manageable and clear. Assign each task a specific time block on your calendar. For example, from 9:00 to 10:30, you might focus solely on drafting an important report. Use timers to reinforce these blocks. Apps like *Focus Keeper* or tools like a simple kitchen timer can help keep you on track.

It works by giving your mind clear boundaries. Time-blocking reduces the pull of external and internal distractions and breaks tasks into bite-sized chunks that your brain can process. It creates a mental agreement during this block of time. "This is what matters most."

Task Batching: Grouping Similar Activities Task batching involves grouping similar tasks to reduce the mental energy spent switching between activities. Shifting from one task to the next can be difficult for an ADHD mind. For example, instead of checking your email sporadically throughout the day, you might dedicate a 30-minute block to responding to all emails at once. Task Batching can include.

Writing tasks: Draft all written materials (emails, reports, proposals) in one sitting. Do the same for all your administration work, completing all small routine tasks (like scheduling, filing, or paying bills back-to-back.

Creative work: Reserve uninterrupted time for brainstorming, designing, or problem-solving.

Prioritization: Knowing What to Focus On ADHD often brings a paradox: ADHD paralysis (knowing where to start) is real and the more tasks there are to do, the more you experience ADHD paralysis. Prioritization tools like the Eisenhower Matrix can help break through this overwhelm by categorizing tasks into four quadrants: You start with the tasks in the "urgent and important" quadrant and work your way down. For added clarity, try color-coding your to-do list based on priority level.

When you constantly switch between different types of tasks, your brain has to keep changing gears. Each time you go from answering emails to writing a report and then back to checking notifications, you lose a bit of momentum. It's like stopping and restarting a car repeatedly—it takes extra effort to get back up to speed.

However, when you batch similar tasks together, your brain doesn't have to work as hard to refocus. Instead of continuously resetting, you remain in one mode of thinking, making it easier to immerse yourself in the task and build momentum naturally.

Think of it like being in "the zone." When you're fully engaged in a task —whether it's writing, problem-solving, or organizing—you enter a flow where everything feels smoother and more effortless. Task batching helps you maintain that state for longer, reducing the mental fatigue that arises from bouncing between unrelated tasks.

Not only does this make your work feel less draining, but it also allows you to accomplish more in less time. You're not wasting energy on constant mental shifts, so you can focus better, work more efficiently, and feel less scattered at the end of the day.

And the best part? You're working with your ADHD brain instead of against it. Rather than forcing yourself to multitask or juggle too many responsibilities at once, you're positioning yourself for success by adapting to the way your brain naturally functions best.

Daily Habits to Reinforce Your Windmill

Mindfulness Practices: Mindfulness helps calm the internal wind by training the brain to focus on the present moment. Even short practices, like a five-minute breathing exercise, can ground your thoughts and improve your ability to redirect attention.

Declutter Your Environment: A streamlined environment makes external distractions easier to manage. Create a workspace that minimizes interruptions by turning off notifications on your phone and computer, using noise-canceling headphones or white noise machines, or keeping your desk clean and free of visual clutter.

Take Regular Breaks: Regular breaks are essential for managing ADHD symptoms and maintaining focus. Use the Pomodoro Technique by working for 25 minutes and then taking a 5-minute break. Taking short, frequent breaks prevents mental fatigue and allows you to reset before diving back in. This is one of my favorites and is very effective for me.

Overcoming Challenges in Building Your Windmill

While these strategies are powerful, building your windmill will require practice and patience. Expect setbacks, just as a windmill must be adjusted to the changing wind, your systems will need fine-tuning as you grow. Common challenges include:

Perfectionism: Waiting for the "perfect" moment or system before starting. Remember, a small step in the right direction will bring you closer to your goal. And here's the secret: there is no "Perfect" time.

Inconsistent Motivation: ADHD often means fluctuating energy levels. Pair high-focus tasks with times when you feel most alert, and reserve low-energy moments for easier activities. It can take a lot of trial and error to discover when those high-focus moments are. But not to worry, I'll help you find your groove.

Embracing the Wind

I know how relentless the wind of ADHD can feel—always pushing, always shifting, making it hard to stay on course. Some days, it feels like no matter how hard you try, your focus scatters in a hundred different directions, and progress seems just out of reach. It's frustrating, exhausting, and at times, downright discouraging.

But here's what I want you to remember: the wind isn't your enemy. It might be unpredictable, even overwhelming at times, but it also carries an incredible force—a power that, when harnessed the right way, can fuel creativity, momentum, and growth. Think of a windmill—it doesn't fight against the wind; it uses it. In the same way, when you start working *with* your mind rather than constantly battling against it, you'll begin to see just how much strength and potential is already within you.

Your distractibility? That's often creativity waiting for the right outlet. Your struggles with organization? Those can turn into productivity when you build systems that *work for you*. The frustration you feel? That energy can be transformed into motivation—momentum to push forward, one step at a time.

I won't tell you it's always easy, but I *will* tell you that it's possible. Every storm holds this duality: challenge and opportunity, chaos and potential. And you, my friend, are capable of taking that storm and turning it into something powerful.

So as we move forward together on this journey, I want you to hold onto this truth: you are not broken, you are not failing—you are learning how to harness your own wind. And once you do, you'll realize just how far it can carry you.

You've got this! And you're not alone.

"Emotions with ADHD are like sudden downpours—intense, overwhelming, and impossible to ignore. But with the right umbrella, you don't have to get soaked."

CHAPTER 3

The Rain and the Umbrella

Imagine a sudden downpour on an otherwise calm day. The sky darkens, the rain comes in torrents, and everything around you becomes harder to see or navigate. This is what emotional regulation challenges feel like for individuals with ADHD—a storm of feelings that can arise without warning, soaking through even the most carefully planned day.

For those with ADHD, emotions aren't just feelings—they can be storms. They come quickly and intensely and often linger longer than they do for others. The ADHD brain struggles to regulate these emotions, making it harder to "shake off" feelings of frustration, excitement, or sadness. Here are some common emotions you might experience:

Heightened Emotional Sensitivity: You feel emotions deeply. Joy can feel like you're on top of the world, while frustration or sadness can feel overwhelming and all-consuming, like being in a pressure cooker. This intensity can lead to rapid emotional shifts soaking through everything like a torrential downpour. Situations that others might shrug off can provoke strong reactions in individuals with ADHD. For example, constructive criticism might feel like a personal attack, or a minor inconvenience might spark disproportionate frustration

Difficulty Returning to a calm state: When a strong emotion is triggered—whether anger, excitement, or anxiety—individuals with ADHD may find it hard to return to a calm, neutral state. It's as if the rain keeps pouring, even when the storm has passed for everyone else.

The cost of unregulated emotional storms seeps into every aspect of life, affecting relationships, work performance, and self-esteem. These challenges often manifest as:

Conflict in Relationships: Intense emotional reactions can lead to misunderstandings or arguments, especially if others don't understand the heightened sensitivity of the ADHD mind.

Workplace Challenges: Managing frustration or stress can make professional settings feel overwhelming, especially in high-pressure environments.

Self-Criticism and Shame: The aftermath of emotional outbursts or impulsive reactions, leaves you experiencing regret or shame, and leads to cycles of self-criticism.

These storms aren't just inconvenient—they can feel isolating and draining, leaving you to wonder if you'll ever find emotional balance.

Building Emotional Resilience

Just as an umbrella protects you from getting drenched in the rain, emotional resilience tools protect you from the downpour of intense feelings. These tools don't stop the rain from falling, but they help you navigate it without becoming overwhelmed. By learning to observe and process emotions rather than reacting to them, you can create a sense of stability even amidst emotional storms.

Build Your Umbrella for Emotional Regulation

If you have ADHD, chances are you feel things *deeply*. Your emotions don't just trickle in gently—they can surge like a powerful storm, intense, unpredictable, and all-consuming.. This heightened emotional sensitivity is often referred to as **Rejection Sensitive Dysphoria (RSD)**, a common but intense experience for many with ADHD. It's that gut-wrenching feeling when criticism, perceived failure, or even a small misunderstanding hits harder than it should—leaving you anxious, discouraged, or even spiraling into self-doubt.

But emotional sensitivity isn't just about pain—it also means you have an incredible capacity for empathy, passion, and deep connection. The challenge is learning how to regulate those emotions so they don't take control.

That's where mindfulness comes in.

Think of emotional regulation like carrying an umbrella in the middle of a storm. You can't always stop the rain from falling, but you *can* protect yourself from being completely drenched. **Mindfulness is that umbrella**—a tool that helps you stay grounded, observe your emotions without getting lost in them, and respond with intention instead of impulse.

In the next section, we'll explore how mindfulness can help you navigate emotional waves with more clarity and calm, making it easier to find balance even when emotions feel overwhelming.

Ways to Practice Mindfulness:

Using grounding techniques, such as focusing on your breath or engaging your senses (e.g., noticing five things you can see, four you can touch, etc.), practicing self-awareness scans to identify where emotions are show-

34

ing up physically—tight shoulders, a clenched jaw, or a racing heart, Journaling as a safe outlet for expressing and exploring emotions. It places the emotion on paper and out of your head. This helps untangle the intensity of feelings and provides clarity about what's driving you. Apps like *Calm* or *Headspace* can also guide you through mindfulness exercises tailored to your emotional regulation. Mindfulness creates a pause between the emotional trigger and your response, giving you space to choose a calmer, more intentional reaction. Here are some techniques that can help:

Writing down emotions: externalizes them, making them feel less overwhelming. It also provides a record you can revisit to identify patterns and triggers over time.

Free-writing: Spend five to ten minutes writing whatever comes to mind without judgment.

Emotion Tracking: Note the events that triggered strong emotions, the feelings that arose, and how you responded.

Gratitude Journaling: List three things you're grateful for. to shift focus toward positive emotions. Do this Daily and Make it a Habit. You'll be glad you did.

Supporting Emotional Well-Being

The body and mind are deeply interconnected. Supporting your physical health can create a stronger foundation for emotional resilience. Key elements for self-care include making new habits. There is a plethora of beneficial practices. It will be up to you to discover which ones are right for you. Some of these may include:

Regular Exercise includes activities such as hiking, running, or even a brisk walk. These activities release endorphins, improving mood and reducing stress.

Balanced Nutrition: Regular, nutritious meals can help regulate emotional highs and lows by maintaining steady blood sugar levels.

Prioritizing Sleep: Restorative sleep improves emotional regulation. Create a bedtime routine to promote consistent, high-quality rest. Without proper sleep, your ADHD symptoms can become intense and unmanageable.

Physical self-care strengthens the body's ability to manage stress, making emotional storms less intense and easier to recover from. Harnessing the storm is a Journey, so give yourself an edge by implementing proper self-care practices.

Expanding the Umbrella for Emotional Growth

Cognitive Behavioral Therapy (CBT): CBT is all about reframing emotional patterns and is a highly effective therapeutic approach for addressing the thought patterns that drive emotional reactivity. CBT identifies negative or distorted thoughts that amplify emotional reactions. (e.g., "I'm always messing up") It reframes these thoughts into more balanced perspectives (e.g., "I made a mistake, but I can learn from it"). It teaches you coping strategies for managing emotional triggers in real-time.

For Example: After a heated argument, CBT might help you recognize that your strong reaction stemmed from an assumption of being unfairly judged, rather than the actual content of the disagreement.

Emotional Check-Ins: Developing Self-Awareness

Regularly checking in with yourself helps you recognize emotions before they escalate. This practice can prevent emotional storms from catching you off guard.

Planned pauses throughout the day to ask, "What am I feeling right now?" Are an effective way to become self-aware Make sure to Label your emotion (e.g., "I feel frustrated" or "I feel anxious") and rate each emotion's intensity on a scale of 1-10. Reflect on what triggered the emotion and whether it requires immediate action or acknowledgment. Building emotional awareness will create a buffer between feeling and reacting, reducing the likelihood of impulsive or disproportionate responses.

Strengthening Your Umbrella: for Long-Term Resilience

Building a Support System Emotional regulation doesn't have to be a solo effort. Surrounding yourself with understanding and supportive individuals can provide an additional layer of resilience.

Who Should You Include in Your Support System? Start with trusted friends or family members who listen without judgment or a Therapist or counselor who offers professional guidance. ADHD support groups are good resources where you can share experiences and learn from others. A strong support system acts as a safety net, helping you navigate emotional challenges with encouragement and perspective.

Practicing Self-Compassion Emotional storms often leave you feeling ashamed or self-critical. Self-compassion shifts this narrative, fostering kindness toward yourself—even in moments of struggle. Use affirmations like, "It's okay to feel this way" or "I'm doing the best I can." Treat yourself as you would a close friend; how would you talk to them if they were struggling? Focus on progress rather than perfection, and celebrate the small victories in emotional growth. It's the small steps that create big change. Self-compassion reduces the shame cycle and reinforces a sense of inner stability and self-worth.

Embracing the Rain

The rain of ADHD, with its emotional intensity, can feel overwhelming, soaking every corner of life. But with the right umbrella, you can weather the storms of emotion, staying dry and grounded even as the rain falls. Mindfulness, journaling, physical self-care, and self-compassion are tools that protect you, allowing you to observe and process emotions without being consumed by them.

As you move forward, remember that emotional storms, like all weather, are temporary. Although the rain may pour, it also nourishes growth, fostering deeper self-awareness, empathy, and resilience. By embracing the rain and using your umbrella, you can transform emotional challenges into a source of strength and understanding.

"Impulsivity is the thunder of ADHD—loud, powerful, and sometimes disruptive. But in the right space, that energy can be transformed into something extraordinary."

CHAPTER 4

Thunder and the Sound Room

Imagine a crack of thunder on a calm day. It's sudden, loud, and demands your attention. For individuals with ADHD, this is what impulsivity feels like—intense and immediate, often driving you to act on an urge without considering the consequences. It can be thrilling and energizing, but it can also lead to decisions that you might later regret.

What Does Impulsivity Look Like?

Impulsivity isn't just about acting without thinking—it's about feeling an overwhelming urge to do something now.

Imagine you're at a store and suddenly need to buy something expensive, even though it isn't within your budget. Or a thought pops into your head during a conversation, and you blurt it out before realizing it might not be the right time. Maybe an idea excites you so much that you abandon what you were working on to pursue it, only to lose interest halfway through.

The Two Sides of Impulsivity

Impulsivity doesn't always look the same. Sometimes, it shows up as **spur-of-the-moment actions**—things you do without thinking, only to regret later. Other times, it's an emotional reaction—a quick burst of frustration, excitement, or hurt that spills out before you have time to process it.

For those with ADHD, impulsivity tends to fall into two main categories:

1. Behavioral Impulsivity: Acting Before Thinking

This is the kind of impulsivity that leads to sudden, unplanned actions—the ones that feel exciting in the moment but may not always be the best decision. It's that urge to take a spontaneous road trip without checking if you have gas, impulsively buying something expensive without thinking about your budget, or abandoning a task mid-way because a new, more exciting idea just popped into your head.

Why does this happen? **Dopamine.** The ADHD brain naturally has lower levels of dopamine, the chemical responsible for motivation and reward. Because of this, it craves stimulation and novelty—anything that provides an instant hit of excitement or satisfaction.

New and risky behaviors **trigger dopamine release**, making impulsive actions feel irresistible in the moment. But once the rush fades, you might be left with the consequences—a half-finished project, an empty bank account, or a plan that sounded great but fell apart because the details weren't considered.

Behavioral impulsivity isn't all bad, though. It's part of what makes ADHD brains so spontaneous, creative, and adventurous. The key is learning how to channel that energy into actions that excite you without causing unnecessary setbacks.2. Emotional Impulsivity: Reacting Before Processing

This form of impulsivity has less to do with actions and more to do with reactions. It's the overwhelming emotional surge that makes you snap at a loved one in frustration, interrupt someone because you're excited, or make a big decision based on how you *feel* in the moment, rather than what's actually best long-term.

People with ADHD often experience emotions intensely—which means anger, sadness, joy, excitement, and frustration can all hit like a tidal wave. When a strong emotion kicks in, it's easy to react before thinking because your brain feels first and processes later.

◆ A slight criticism might feel like a personal attack, making you lash out defensively before realizing the person didn't mean any harm.

◆ A new idea might fill you with excitement, leading you to drop everything else to pursue it—only to lose steam later.

◆ A small setback might feel like the end of the world, causing you to give up instead of reassessing the situation.

This emotional intensity is part of **Rejection Sensitive Dysphoria (RSD)**, a common experience for those with ADHD. It's why some reactions feel bigger, stronger, and harder to control than they might for others.

But just like behavioral impulsivity, emotional impulsivity can be managed and redirected. The goal isn't to suppress your emotions but to create space between feeling and reacting—so you can respond instead of regret.

It's important to note that understanding both types of impulsivity is the first step in managing them. Whether it's pausing before making a big purchase or taking a breath before responding in anger, learning to insert even a small moment of reflection can make all the difference.

In the next section, we'll dive into practical strategies for working *with* impulsivity instead of letting it control you. When you learn to harness the energy of impulsivity, you can turn it into a strength instead of a struggle.

Why does impulsivity happen? The ADHD brain craves stimulation, and impulsivity often feels like the fastest way to satisfy that craving. This is tied to differences in how the brain processes dopamine, the chemical that drives reward and motivation. Impulsive actions provide a quick burst of dopamine, which can feel incredibly satisfying in the moment but might not always lead to the best outcomes.

The Consequences of Thunderous Impulsivity

When impulsivity is left unchecked, it can create ripples that affect every aspect of life. Impulsivity can also Harm Personal relationships by blurting out hurtful words in the heat of the moment or making snap decisions that can potentially strain friendships, partnerships, and family dynamics.

These impulsive choices can hinder career growth by speaking out of turn, abandoning a project, or missing deadlines. Impulsivity can also lead to financial and safety risks like overspending, gambling, or engaging in unsafe activities without considering the potential harm.

The thunder of ADHD's impulsivity is not inherently negative—it's a force of energy and spontaneity that, when directed wisely, can fuel creativity, innovation, and boldness. The key is learning how to ground this energy and channel its power into constructive, manageable outlets.

The Sound Room: Channeling Impulsivity

Think about the way a **sound room** works. When thunder crashes outside, the walls don't stop the sound from existing—they absorb and soften it, controlling how it moves through the space. The thunder still happens, but inside the sound room, it becomes more manageable.

This is exactly how we should approach impulsivity. The goal isn't to silence it completely—it's part of who you are, part of what makes you spontaneous, creative, and full of energy. Instead of trying to fight against it, the key is to redirect that energy in a way that serves you rather than disrupts your life.

Impulsivity can be a powerful force when it's channeled with intention. It can spark bold ideas, fuel passion projects, and lead to exciting new experiences—but only if there's some structure to guide it. Without that structure, impulsive energy can easily turn into regretful decisions, scattered efforts, and frustration over unfinished tasks.

That's where practical tools come in. By creating space for safe, structured spontaneity, you can make impulsivity work *for* you instead of against you. In the next section, we'll explore ways to harness that energy and give it a clear direction so you can enjoy the thrill of impulsivity without the downsides. Let's dive in.

Creating Structured Spontaneity

Impulsivity thrives in unstructured moments—those times when you suddenly feel the urge to act on a whim without a plan in place. That's when it's easiest to make snap decisions that might feel exciting at the moment but later leave you frustrated, overwhelmed, or dealing with consequences you didn't anticipate.

But here's the thing: impulsivity isn't *inherently* a bad thing. In fact, when used wisely, it can fuel creativity, adventure, and new experiences that add richness to your life. The trick is giving that impulsive energy a place to go—a way to enjoy the thrill of spontaneity without letting it take over.

This is where structured spontaneity comes in. It's all about pre-setting opportunities for impulsive behaviors in ways that minimize risk and maximize satisfaction. Instead of trying to suppress the urge to be spontaneous, you create safe outlets where that energy can flow without throwing your priorities off track.

Let's talk about two simple strategies to help you do just that.

The "Impulse Bucket" Technique

Sometimes, impulsivity strikes because your brain needs stimulation. Instead of letting that urge pull you into something that might not be the best choice, why not have a go-to list of safe, exciting alternatives?

That's what the Impulse Bucket is—a list of low-risk, high-reward activities you can turn to whenever you feel the itch to do something spontaneous. The idea is to channel impulsivity into an outlet that brings enjoyment and novelty without negative consequences.

Here are a few ideas to add to your Impulse Bucket:

◆ **Try a new recipe or hobby**—Something you can start *right now* without a long commitment.

◆ **Explore a new walking trail**—A quick adventure that satisfies curiosity and movement.

◆ **Visit an unfamiliar park or bookstore**—New environments provide fresh stimulation without major consequences.

- **Watch a highly recommended documentary or read a short article**—Something engaging, interesting, and immediately rewarding.

- **Do a small, creative project**—Sketch something, journal a spontaneous thought, or start a puzzle.

Having an Impulse Bucket means that instead of feeling frustrated or guilty for acting on a whim, you have a list of safe, fun, and productive ways to satisfy that urge.

Pre-Approval for Impulsive Decisions

One of the biggest risks of ADHD impulsivity is making big decisions on the spot—whether it's overspending, jumping into new commitments too quickly, or saying "yes" to something before thinking it through. The excitement and dopamine rush can make it hard to stop and evaluate.

A great way to work *with* this tendency instead of against it is to set pre-approved limits—boundaries that allow you to be impulsive but in a controlled and intentional way.

Create a "fun budget" for spontaneous purchases. Instead of impulsively buying something expensive and regretting it later, give yourself a set amount of money each month for guilt-free, unplanned purchases. That way, you still get the thrill of spontaneity but without financial stress.

Designate a time window for impulse-driven adventures. Maybe you love last-minute road trips or spontaneous activities, but they sometimes get in the way of responsibilities. Instead of saying "no" to spontaneity, schedule it. Set aside a time—like Saturday afternoons—as your designated "yes" time for impulsive ideas. This keeps the excitement while protecting your time and commitments.

Give yourself a "pause button" for big decisions. If you feel the urge to make a major impulse decision (like quitting a job, starting a big project, or making a large purchase), create a rule that says,

"I'll wait 24 hours before acting on it."

This small delay can help your brain step out of the impulsive moment and make sure the decision still feels right after the initial dopamine rush fades.

Why Structured Spontaneity Works

These techniques allow you to work with your impulsivity instead of fighting against it, creating opportunities to enjoy spontaneity without the negative fallout.

- The Impulse Bucket gives you a go-to list of stimulating, rewarding activities that won't derail your responsibilities.
- Pre-approved impulsivity allows you to enjoy the excitement of unplanned decisions while keeping your finances, time, and commitments in check.

With the right systems in place, impulsivity becomes a tool, not a burden. You don't have to lose the excitement of spontaneous actions—you just need to create space where they can thrive without causing chaos.

So go ahead and embrace your spontaneous side, but do so in a way that adds value to your life rather than diminishing it.

Building Pause-and-Plan Habits

The "pause and plan" method helps individuals insert a moment of re-flection between an impulse and an action. This little pause gives you time to process the impulsive behavior. Allowing you to analyze your decisions and decide if they align with your Goals. A planned pause can make the difference between a productive choice and a regrettable one.

Techniques for Pausing

Practice the **5-Second Rule**: When you feel an impulse, count to five before acting. Ask yourself whether the action aligns with your goals.

Use physical reminders, such as a bracelet or sticky note, to pause when making decisions. There are many other ways to remind yourself to pause and evaluate. Find what works for you.

Quick Self-Check Questions:

1. "Why do I want to do this?"
2. "What will happen if I act on this impulse?"
3. "Is there a better way to satisfy this urge?"

Designing a Dopamine-Friendly Environment

Impulsivity is often a symptom of the ADHD brain's search for dopamine. By designing an environment that naturally supports healthy dopamine regulation, you can reduce the need for risky or impulsive behavior.

Incorporate Frequent Rewards: Break tasks or chunk them into smaller steps and reward yourself for completing each one. This provides regular dopamine boosts without the need for impulsive diversions.

Engage in Physical Activity: Exercise, especially high-intensity activities like running or dancing, increases dopamine levels and reduces restlessness, creating a distraction and a gap. This gives you space to re-evaluate the action.

Create a Stimulation Toolbox: Fill a small box or digital list with quick, satisfying activities that provide novelty, such as solving a puzzle, exploring a new app, or listening to an energizing song.

Long-Term Strategies for Grounding Impulsivity

Developing Self-Awareness: Understanding your triggers is key to managing impulsivity. A journal or digital log is a great tool for tracking patterns. Journal entries may include writing, noting what situations or emotions spark impulsive behaviors, or noting how often I feel boredom, stress, or overstimulation. Reflecting on these patterns can help you anticipate and prepare for future impulses.

Practicing Emotional Regulation: Emotional impulsivity often accompanies behavioral impulsivity. Practicing mindfulness or cognitive behavioral therapy (CBT) can help calm emotional storms before they drive impulsive actions. Try using techniques such as:

Mindful Breathing and Reframing: When emotions run high, take slow, deep breaths to center yourself. Practice reframing negative thoughts, such as replacing "I need to act now" with "I can revisit this idea later."

Setting Boundaries and Accountability: External accountability can serve as an effective "Sound Room" for impulsivity. Share goals with trusted friends or family who know your intentions and can gently remind you of boundaries.

Use Tools for Oversight: Apps like *You Need a Budget* (for finances) or *Trello* (for task management) provide structure and oversight for impulsive decisions.

Body Doubling is a technique in which you work alongside another person to improve Focus, motivation, and productivity. It involves having a partner or "body double" present while performing a task, such as studying, writing, or completing household chores. The body double can provide companionship, accountability, and a sense of structure. Body doubling is a common practice for people with ADHD and is very effective in helping them stay on track and complete tasks more efficiently.

Embracing the Thunder

The thunder of impulsivity is a defining feature of ADHD. Intense bursts of energy and action can feel exhilarating but can also be destabilizing. By using tools like structured spontaneity, the pause-and-plan method, and a dopamine-friendly environment, you can ground this energy without losing its vibrancy.

As you implement these strategies, remember that impulsivity isn't a flaw. It's a natural part of how your brain seeks stimulation and novelty. The goal isn't to silence the thunder but to harness its power, transforming impulsive tendencies into opportunities for creativity, connection, and growth.

Each element of the storm carries both challenge and potential. With the right tools, you can embrace the thunder as a source of energy that drives you forward, creating a life where spontaneity and intention coexist in harmony.

"Hyper-focus is the lightning of ADHD—electrifying and intense. If you can direct it, you can light up the world."

CHAPTER 5

Lightning and the Lightning Rod

Imagine a bolt of lightning streaking across the sky—sudden, powerful, and awe-inspiring. It lights up everything in its path, but it's fleeting, unpredictable, and, if left uncontrolled, potentially destructive. For individuals with ADHD, hyper-focus, creative bursts, and mental energy spikes are much like lightning. These moments of intense focus and creativity can lead to extraordinary achievements, but they can also leave you feeling drained, burnt out, or overwhelmed by unfinished projects.

What Does ADHD's Lightning Feel Like?

Imagine your mind as a stormy sky, where bursts of lightning flash across the horizon—sudden, powerful, and impossible to ignore. That's what ADHD's mental energy can feel like. At some moments, your brain locks into hyper-focus, shutting out the world as you dive deeply into a task. Other times, a surge of creative bursts floods your mind with new ideas, all fighting for attention at once. And then there are mental energy spikes, where your brain feels like it's running at full speed—exciting, yet unpredictable.

These mental lightning strikes are a core part of ADHD. They can be exhilarating, leading to moments of incredible productivity, insight, and achievement. But if left unchecked, they can also leave you mentally drained, overwhelmed, and surrounded by unfinished tasks. Let's take a closer look at how each one works—and how they all connect.

Hyper-Focus: Deep, Intense, and Unbreakable

Hyper-focus is one of ADHD's greatest paradoxes. While distractibility is often associated with ADHD, hyper-focus is the opposite—it's an intense state of absorption where you become completely locked into whatever you're doing. Time seems to vanish. You forget to eat, stretch, or even go to the bathroom because your mind is fully engaged.

In this state, your productivity can soar. You might finish an entire project in one sitting, research a topic for hours without stopping, or master a skill at lightning speed. It's like your brain switches into supercharged mode, allowing you to block out distractions and channel all your energy into one thing.

But hyper-focus can also have a downside. Because you're so absorbed, you might neglect other important tasks, forget about responsibilities, or push yourself to the point of exhaustion. The key to harnessing hyper-focus is learning how to control when and where it happens so it works *for* you instead of against you.

Creative Bursts: A Flood of Ideas with No Off-Switch

Then there are the creative bursts—those moments when your brain suddenly overflows with ideas, each one as exciting as the last. You're brainstorming, problem-solving, or imagining something new, and it feels like your mind is on fire with possibility.

These bursts can be brilliant. Many people with ADHD are incredibly innovative thinkers, able to connect ideas in unique ways that others might not see. This is why so many artists, entrepreneurs, and inventors thrive with ADHD—because their minds can generate fresh, out-of-the-box ideas at lightning speed.

The challenge? There are often too many ideas at once. It's like trying to drink from a firehose—you're hit with so much inspiration that it becomes overwhelming. You might start multiple projects but struggle to finish them, or you feel paralyzed and unsure of which idea to pursue first. If hyper-focus is about getting stuck on one thing, then creative bursts are about wanting to chase everything all at once.

Learning how to capture and organize these ideas is key. Instead of feeling pulled in a hundred directions, you can develop systems that allow you to store and revisit ideas later, so you don't lose their potential but also don't become overwhelmed by them.

Mental Energy Spikes: The ADHD Brain on Full Blast

The final piece of ADHD's lightning is the mental energy spike—a surge of motivation, excitement, or pure brain power that makes you feel like you can take on the world. Your mind is firing on all cylinders, you're filled with enthusiasm, and everything seems possible.

These spikes can be incredibly productive and energizing. When they hit at the right time, they help you power through work, start new projects, or dive into learning something new. You feel unstoppable—until, suddenly, the energy disappears as fast as it came.

That's the tricky part: Mental energy spikes are unpredictable. One moment, you're charged up and ready to go; the next, you crash, feeling drained and frustrated because you can't sustain the momentum. It's like a rollercoaster of motivation—one that can leave you feeling guilty for not being able to keep up the same pace.

The key here isn't trying to force the energy to last forever but rather to work with the natural ebb and flow of your mental energy. By recognizing when these spikes happen and learning to pace yourself, you can make the most of them without burning out.

The Reason Hyper-focus, creative bursts, and mental energy spikes connect is simply because they are all part of the same storm. They can show up separately, but often, they feed into each other:

⚡ You get a creative burst, filling your mind with exciting ideas.

⚡ One of those ideas triggers hyper-focus, locking you in for hours.

⚡ mental energy spike fuels your momentum—until it suddenly crashes.

This cycle can be both a gift and a challenge. When the lightning is harnessed correctly, it can lead to incredible accomplishments, deep work, and groundbreaking ideas. However, if unmanaged, it can result in unfinished projects, burnout, and frustration.

The good news? You don't have to fight the lightning—you just need the right tools to channel it.

In the next section, we'll explore how to build your own lightning rod—a set of strategies to help you capture the power of ADHD's mental energy without letting it burn you out.

These lightning strikes aren't inherently bad, and they're one of ADHD's greatest strengths. But without direction, they can lead to burnout, missed priorities, or a trail of incomplete tasks.

While these challenges are real, ADHD's lightning is also one of its greatest strengths. When channeled effectively, this trait allows individuals to produce work of exceptional quality, creativity, and innovation. Hyper-focus is not a weakness—it's a superpower waiting to be harnessed.

A lightning rod channels the raw energy of lightning into something productive and safe. Similarly, with the right strategies, you can harness your hyper-focus and creative bursts to work for you, not against you.

The first step to managing hyper-focus is understanding when it occurs and embracing it as a natural part of the brain's functioning. Hyper-focus isn't something to suppress—it's a strength that, when guided, can lead to extraordinary results.

Signs You're Entering Hyper-Focus

Hyper-focus isn't something that announces itself with a flashing neon sign—it just happens. One minute, you're sitting down to start a task, and the next, hours have passed in what feels like minutes. Time slips away without you realizing it.

When you're in this state, the world around you seems to fade. Distractions that normally pull at your attention—your phone buzzing, someone calling your name, hunger, even the need to use the bathroom —barely register. It's like your brain has flipped a switch, locking onto a single point of focus with laser precision. You're completely immersed— whether it's writing, designing, researching, or even playing a video game, everything else fades into the background.

But hyper-focus isn't just about being absorbed in something. It often comes with a sense of heightened clarity, creativity, or productivity. Your mind feels sharp, ideas flow easily, and you may produce some of your best work. It's why so many people with ADHD see hyper-focus as a superpower—because when it's directed at the right things, it can lead to incredible results.

The problem? It's easy to get lost in hyper-focus without realizing it's happening. That's when it can become a double-edged sword—pushing you to work past the point of exhaustion, skip meals, neglect other responsibilities, or hyper-fixate on something that isn't a priority.

That's why self-awareness is so important. The more you recognize the signs of hyper-focus as they begin, the better you can guide it, rather than letting it control you.

How to Use This Awareness

Understanding when and how hyper-focus happens gives you the power to harness it intentionally. Instead of getting swept away by it, you can start using it on your terms, making sure it fuels your goals rather than pulling you away from them. Let's explore how to do just that.

Keep a journal or note when hyper-focus occurs. Pay attention to patterns, such as specific times of day, tasks, or environments that trigger it.

Plan high-focus tasks during times when you're most likely to enter hyper-focus. For example, if you notice you're most productive in the mornings, reserve that time for your most important projects.

For Example, Emma, a graphic designer, noticed she entered hyper-focus late at night while working on creative projects. Instead of fighting this natural rhythm, she adjusted her schedule to tackle her design work in the evenings and reserved her mornings for administrative tasks. By aligning her tasks with her natural energy, she was able to produce her best work while avoiding burnout.

Setting Boundaries to Avoid Burnout

Hyper-focus can feel like a superpower, allowing you to lock into a task with incredible intensity and produce some of your best work. But here's the thing—it's also mentally and physically draining if you don't set limits. When you get lost in hyper-focus, it's easy to forget basic needs like eating, stretching, or even drinking water. That's why creating structure around your focus sessions is so important—it helps you stay productive without running yourself into the ground. Here are a few simple but powerful ways to keep hyper-focus working for you instead of against you:

1. Use Timers to Keep Focus Manageable

One of the biggest risks of hyper-focus is losing track of time completely. Before you know it, hours have passed, and you realize you haven't moved, eaten, or taken a break. This can lead to burnout, tension headaches, and exhaustion, making it harder to function once you finally snap out of it. *That's why timers are your best friend!*

Using structured time intervals, like the **Pomodoro Technique** (25 minutes of work followed by a 5-minute break), helps you stay focused without overextending yourself. These built-in breaks serve as gentle reminders to pause, stretch, grab a snack, or just breathe for a moment. If 25 minutes feels too short, adjust it—maybe you work best in 45-minute blocks with 10-minute breaks. The key is finding a rhythm that helps you stay productive without draining yourself.

You can also use alarms or reminders for essential self-care, like:

- A hydration reminder: "Drink a glass of water!"
- A movement break: "Get up, stretch, and walk around for a minute."
- A reset timer: "Step away and check in with yourself—do you need a break?"

These simple reminders interrupt hyper-focus just enough to help you stay balanced and avoid burnout.

2. Establish Routines to Create Natural Stopping Points

One of the challenges with hyper-focus is that it doesn't come with an "off switch." You might keep going and going, unable to stop even when you know you need to. That's why clear starting and stopping rituals can be incredibly helpful.

Think of it as setting bookends for your focus time. Just as a morning routine helps signal the start of your day, a focus-starting ritual tells your brain, *"Okay, it's time to dive in."* And just as important, a focus-ending ritual helps you transition out of hyper-focus smoothly instead of crashing.

Ideas for starting a focus session:

Light a candle or use a specific essential oil scent to signal focus time or play a particular song or sound (like lo-fi beats or nature sounds) to create a sensory cue. Write down your top three priorities to clarify what you're working on. Here are ways to end your session and step away:

Stretch or do a short movement break to loosen up your body.
Journal for a minute to reflect on what you accomplished.
Power down your workspace (close tabs, turn off your computer, clean your desk).

When you create intentional start and stop points, it becomes easier to manage hyper-focus instead of feeling like it's controlling you.

3. Plan Recovery Time to Recharge Your Brain

After a deep hyper-focus session, you might feel mentally drained, even if you didn't realize it while working. This is because hyper-focus demands a lot of mental energy, and if you don't give yourself time to recharge, you risk burning out before you even notice it happening.

The best way to prevent this? Schedule recovery time right after periods of intense focus. You can take a short walk outside—Fresh air and movement help reset your mind, Practice deep breathing or mindfulness —Even just five minutes can be grounding, engage in a fun, low-effort activity—Something enjoyable but not mentally demanding (like listening to music, doodling, or playing a simple game) or one of my favorites,

Spend time with loved ones—Social interaction helps pull you out of work mode and reconnect with reality. Think of these recovery moments as fuel stops for your brain—they keep you going without running on empty.

Boundaries matter because it's easy to think, *"But I'm getting so much done! Why would I stop?"*—especially when you're in the middle of a hyper-focused work session. But the reality is, if you don't set boundaries, hyper-focus will eventually drain you, making it harder to be productive in the long run. They aren't restrictions—they're safeguards. They protect your physical and mental well-being, ensuring that your most brilliant moments don't come at the cost of exhaustion, missed meals, or burnout.

So the next time you feel yourself falling into deep hyper-focus, try implementing just one of these techniques. With practice, you'll learn to harness your focus without letting it control you—and that's where the real magic happens. Capturing Creativity Without Losing Momentum

Creative bursts are one of ADHD's most exciting traits. However, the challenge is channeling those bursts into actionable outcomes rather than letting them overwhelm you. Here are some techniques that can help channel that energy:

Idea Notebooks: Keep a small notebook or use a digital tool like Evernote or Notion to jot down ideas as they come to you. This way, you won't feel pressured to act on every idea immediately.

Prioritize and Plan: Once you've captured your ideas, take time to prioritize which ones align with your current goals. Use simple frameworks like checklists or the Eisenhower Matrix to decide what to pursue now and what to revisit later.

Collaborate for Accountability: Share your creative ideas with trusted colleagues, mentors, or friends. They are your support group and can help you refine, motivate, and see your ideas through a different lens.

For example, Josh, a marketing professional, often experienced creative bursts while brainstorming campaigns. Instead of acting on every idea right away, he started keeping a dedicated "idea list." At the end of each week, he reviewed his list and chose one or two ideas to develop further. This approach helped him stay focused while preserving his creativity.

Creating an Environment That Supports Hyper-focus

Your surroundings play a bigger role in your focus than you might realize. When you're in a cluttered, noisy, or visually overwhelming space, your brain has to work overtime to filter out distractions. Even if you're hyper-focused on a task, background chaos—whether it's piles of paperwork, a cluttered desk, or notifications popping up on your screen—can pull at your attention, making it harder to stay locked in.

On the flip side, when your environment is designed to support deep focus, it becomes much easier to harness your mental energy without constantly fighting off distractions. A well-organized space acts like a mental cue, signaling to your brain, *"This is where focus happens."* It can help you settle into work faster, stay immersed longer, and minimize the mental fatigue that comes from constantly shifting attention.

This doesn't mean you need a Pinterest-perfect office or an expensive workspace setup. What matters most is intentionality—creating a space that supports your brain's natural tendencies rather than working against them. Maybe that means having a clean, clutter-free desk, adjusting your lighting to make the space feel inviting, or even adding elements that inspire creativity, like a favorite piece of artwork or a plant. For some, background noise, like white noise or instrumental music, can help maintain focus, while for others, absolute silence is key. The important thing is to experiment and find what works best for you.

A distraction-free space isn't just about eliminating the things that pull your attention away—it's also about designing an environment that actively encourages focus and engagement. When your space is set up to work *with* your brain rather than against it, you'll find it much easier to enter and sustain hyper-focus without feeling overwhelmed or overstimulated.

Tips for Creating a Focus-Friendly Environment

Your environment has a direct impact on your ability to focus, especially when you have an ADHD brain that's highly sensitive to distractions. A well-designed workspace doesn't just help you concentrate—it actively encourages deep focus by minimizing interruptions and maximizing mental clarity. When your surroundings support your brain's natural tendencies, it becomes much easier to enter and sustain hyper-focus without constantly battling against external and internal distractions.

Here are a few ways to create an environment that works for you rather than against you.

Declutter Your Space

A cluttered workspace can lead to a cluttered mind. When too many things compete for your attention—stacks of papers, random objects, tangled cords—your brain has to work harder to filter out distractions. Even if you think you're ignoring the mess, it's still taking up *mental real estate* in the background, making it harder to stay fully engaged in your work.

Clearing your space doesn't mean it has to be sterile or empty, but rather intentional. Keep only what you need within arm's reach, and find designated spots for everything else. If something doesn't serve a purpose or inspire you, it's probably just visual noise. A clean, organized workspace helps your brain relax into focus without the mental drag of unnecessary distractions.

Incorporate Inspiring Elements

While reducing clutter is important, a completely bare space can feel uninspiring. Your workspace should be functional but also feel inviting and energizing—a place you *want* to spend time in.

Adding elements that inspire you—whether it's a piece of artwork, a small plant, or a warm-toned lamp—can make your environment feel more personal and engaging. For some, having a vision board with goals and motivational quotes serves as a reminder of what they're working toward. Others might find that natural lighting or soft ambient lighting makes a big difference in how they feel throughout the day.

Find what sparks positive energy and motivation for you. If something makes you feel *calm, inspired, or excited to work*, it's worth including in your space.

Use Productivity Tools to Minimize Distractions

Let's be real—one of the biggest obstacles to staying focused isn't just the physical space around you but the digital distractions that constantly compete for your attention. Your phone, email notifications, and endless internet rabbit holes can quickly derail even the best intentions. That's where productivity tools can help.

Apps like Forest encourage you to stay off your phone by "growing" a virtual tree while you work—if you leave the app, the tree dies. It's a simple but effective way to gamify focus and create a sense of accountability. Focus@Will is another great tool that provides background music scientifically designed to enhance concentration and reduce distractions. If silence makes it harder for you to stay engaged, having the right background noise can be a game-changer.

If you find yourself constantly switching between tabs or checking notifications, try using website blockers like Freedom or Cold Turkey to temporarily disable access to distracting sites. These small adjustments can make a huge difference in keeping your mind on track and fully immersed in your work.

A Well-Designed Environment is an Invisible Advantage

The goal isn't just to create a workspace that *looks* nice—it's to create an intentional environment that supports your focus, energy, and productivity. When your surroundings are thoughtfully set up to reduce distractions and encourage deep work, your brain doesn't have to fight as hard to stay engaged.

Think of your environment as a silent partner in your productivity. When it works *for* you, everything feels smoother and more effortless. Take the time to design a space that makes focus feel natural, and you'll be amazed at how much easier it becomes to channel your energy into meaningful work.

The Cost of Untamed Lightning

While hyper-focus and creative bursts are powerful, they can become overwhelming if left unchecked. Hyper-focus is a gift and, at the same time, a double-edged sword if left unchecked. Untamed Lightning can pose several risks, such as:

Burnout: Losing yourself in hyper-focus can mean skipping meals, sleep, or breaks, leaving you drained and unable to sustain your energy.

Incomplete Projects: The initial excitement of a creative burst can fade quickly, leaving you with half-finished ideas or tasks.

Missed Priorities: Hyper-focus can pull your attention away from pressing responsibilities, creating a cycle of guilt and frustration.

Overcommitting: The thrill of hyper-focus can lead to saying yes to too many projects or ideas, spreading yourself too thin.

Emotional Strain: The intensity of hyper-focus can create high expectations, which can lead to frustration or disappointment when energy levels wane.

But here's the good news: just as lightning can be harnessed with a lightning rod, your ADHD energy can be directed in ways that maximize its potential while protecting your well-being.

A Strategy for Channeling the Lightning

One of the best ways to harness hyper-focus is by setting clear, structured goals that help direct your energy in meaningful ways. Hyper-focus can be an incredible gift when it's aligned with your priorities, but without direction, it's easy to pour that energy into things that don't actually move you forward. That's where **SMART goals** come in.

SMART goals—**S**pecific, **M**easurable, **A**chievable, **R**elevant, and **T**imebound—help turn big ideas into clear, actionable steps. They also make it easier to stay focused without getting lost in endless possibilities. When hyper-focus kicks in, these goals act as a guiding framework, ensuring that your energy is spent on something that will bring real results.

Let's break it down.

Specific goals leave no room for vagueness. Instead of saying, *"I want to be more productive,"* you'd say, *"I want to finish drafting my business proposal by Friday."* This eliminates ambiguity, giving your brain a clear target to lock onto.

Measurable goals help you track progress. Instead of setting a vague intention like, *"I want to write more,"* try, *"I will write 1,000 words per day for the next five days."* Measurable goals make it easy to see whether you're moving forward or need to adjust your approach.

Achievable goals should be challenging, but still realistic. If your goal is too big or unrealistic, it can quickly become overwhelming, leading to frustration and burnout. Instead of saying, *"I'll write an entire book in a week,"* break it down into smaller milestones, like, *"I'll outline the first three chapters this week."*

Relevant goals ensure that you're focusing on what matters. It's easy to get swept up in hyper-focus on things that *feel* productive but don't actually align with your larger goals. Before committing to a goal, ask yourself: *"Is this moving me in the right direction?"* If not, it might be a distraction in disguise.

Time-bound goals have a clear deadline. Hyper-focus tends to ignore time, so without a set timeframe, tasks can stretch on indefinitely. Giving yourself a deadline—*"I'll finish my project proposal by the end of the month"*—creates a sense of urgency, helping you stay on track.

When hyper-focus strikes, SMART goals act as a lightning rod, channeling that intense energy into focused, meaningful action. Instead of getting lost in a sea of scattered ideas or unfinished projects, you'll have a clear path forward, making the most of your ADHD superpower without burning out.

Celebrate Progress: Take time to acknowledge and celebrate what you've achieved during those periods of hyper-focus. This will reinforce positive behavior and provide a sense of satisfaction, reducing the ever-present need to chase constant novelty.

Pair Hyper-focus with Downtime To better maintain your energy, balance intense focus with intentional rest. Engage in activities that promote relaxation and recovery, such as mindfulness exercises, physical activity, or hobbies that don't require high levels of mental energy.

Embracing the Lightning

As you continue your journey, remember that every element of the storm holds the potential for transformation. Lightning, with its power and intensity, isn't just a challenge—it's a beacon of what makes your mind extraordinary. With the right tools, you can direct your energy to illuminate your path and inspire those around you.

Remember: lightning isn't something to fear or suppress—it's a gift to be celebrated. With the right lightning rod, you can channel its power into meaningful achievements, transforming moments of brilliance into lasting success. So, the next time lightning strikes, don't panic. Take a deep breath, grab your lightning rod, and let your brilliance shine.

"Remember, the fog is temporary. Each small step you take clears the path just a little more. With patience, compassion, and your compass in hand, you'll move through the uncertainty and into clarity, one moment at a time."

Chapter 6

The Fog and the Compass

Imagine walking through a dense fog. You can't see what's ahead, everything feels muffled, and even taking a single step feels uncertain. For individuals with ADHD, this fog isn't just a passing moment—it can be a daily reality. It's the mental cloudiness that makes it hard to focus, prioritize, or make decisions. It's the feeling of being stuck, unsure of where to begin or how to move forward. The fog of ADHD can take many forms, but here are some common experiences:

Memory Challenges: Forgetting where you left your keys, missing appointments, or losing track of details you were sure you'd remember.

Decision Paralysis: Feeling overwhelmed when faced with too many choices, unable to decide what to do next.

Unclear Priorities: Struggling to determine which tasks matter most leads to procrastinating or wasting time on unimportant activities.

Imagine you have a day off and a long to-do list. You sit down to start working, but instead of feeling productive, you find yourself scrolling through social media or reorganizing your desk for the fifth time. By the end of the day, you're frustrated because nothing important got done. That's the fog in action—it clouds your ability to see a clear path forward.

The Cost of Living in the Fog

Living in the fog isn't just frustrating—it's disorienting, exhausting, and deeply discouraging. It's that feeling of constantly trying to move forward but never being quite sure where you're going. It's knowing there are things you need to do but feeling stuck and unable to begin. It's wanting to make progress but getting caught in a cycle of delays, distractions, and doubt that leaves you feeling like you're falling behind.

Procrastination

People often mistake procrastination for laziness, but if you've ever been caught in the fog, you know that's not the case. It's not that you *don't* want to get things done—you do. It's just that the path forward feels too unclear, too overwhelming. Your brain searches for the starting point, but everything feels tangled. The longer you put it off, the heavier the task becomes, like a weight pressing down on you. And even though you *know* the longer you wait, the harder it will be, you still can't seem to break through the inertia.

Avoidance

When the fog is thick, avoidance becomes the easy way out. Not because you don't care, but because facing the unknown feels impossible. Instead of tackling the difficult task, you retreat into distractions—binge-watching TV, scrolling endlessly on your phone, or diving into something that *feels* productive but isn't actually what needs to be done. For a little while, it provides relief. Eventually, the reality of what's left undone catches up with you, bringing guilt, anxiety, and even deeper frustration.

Self-Doubt

The worst part of living in the fog is what it does to your self-belief. When you're constantly struggling to move forward, it's easy to start questioning yourself. *Why can't I just do this? What's wrong with me? Why does everyone else seem to have it figured out while I'm stuck in the same place?* The longer you stay in this cycle, the more your confidence erodes, making it even harder to break free.

But here's the truth, the fog is not permanent. It may feel overwhelming right now, but this moment—this feeling of being stuck—is not a reflection of your potential. You are not broken. You are not failing. You are learning how to navigate in a way that works for you.

And the good news? There's a way forward. With the right tools, your "compass" can guide you through the haze, helping you regain clarity, direction, and momentum. Even if you can't see the whole path, taking one step at a time is enough. Every small action—every effort to push forward—brings you closer to breaking through.

You don't have to stay lost in the fog—keep going— You will find your way.

The Compass: Finding Direction in the Fog

Just as a compass helps you navigate through a foggy landscape, ADHD navigation tools can guide you through mental cloudiness. These tools won't eliminate the fog, but they'll give you the clarity you need and steer you toward your goals, reduce overwhelm, and maintain focus on the things that matter most. Take one step at a time.

When you're living with ADHD, "out of sight, out of mind" isn't just a saying—it's reality. Visual reminders can act as guideposts, ensuring you don't lose track of important tasks or goals.

Use Visual Reminders

Use sticky notes on your bathroom mirror or computer screen to list your top three priorities for the day. Keep a whiteboard in a prominent spot to jot down deadlines, appointments, or reminders or color-code tasks by urgency. For example, use red for "must do today," yellow for "this week," and green for "when there's time."

For example, Chris, a college student with ADHD, struggled to remember his assignments. He started using a large calendar on his wall where he wrote down all his deadlines. Each morning, he glanced at it to plan his day. This simple habit helped him stay on track and reduced his last-minute stress.

Remember visual reminders externalize memory, taking the burden off your brain and giving you constant prompts to stay on track.

Daily Checklists: Breaking Through Procrastination

When you're lost in the fog, a checklist can be your compass, breaking overwhelming tasks into small, manageable steps. How to Create a Checklist:

Brain Dump: Write down everything you need to do, no matter how small. Group similar tasks together, like emails, errands, or phone calls.

Break big tasks into smaller steps. For example, instead of "clean the house," write "tidy the living room," "vacuum," and "do laundry."

For Example, Alex, an entrepreneur, often felt overwhelmed by his growing to-do list. By creating a checklist every morning and tackling one item at a time, he felt a sense of accomplishment and reduced his anxiety about the day ahead.

There are many great tools and methods for checklists. They provide structure and clarity, helping you focus on one task at a time instead of feeling paralyzed by everything you need to do.

Apps like *Todoist*, *Motion*, or *Trello* provide digital platforms for organizing tasks. There are many apps available. Pick one that works for you. Paper planners or notebooks work well for those who prefer tactile methods.

Checklists transform vague goals into actionable steps, providing a clear path forward and reducing the tendency to procrastinate.

The Decision Matrix is a great tool when you can't seem to get past making a decision (Analysis Paralysis)

When every option feels equally important, it's easy to freeze. A decision matrix helps you weigh your options and make choices with confidence.

Using the Decision Matrix

Sometimes, making a decision feels impossible. It's not because you don't care or because you're avoiding responsibility—it's because every option feels equally important, and your brain keeps running in circles, weighing the pros and cons without ever reaching a conclusion.

I've been there more times than I can count. I've sat at my desk, staring at two or three possible choices, feeling completely stuck. No matter how much I thought about it, my mind wouldn't land on an answer. Instead, I'd go over the same factors again and again, each one seeming to cancel out the other. That's the weight of analysis paralysis—the fear of making the *wrong* decision keeps you from making *any* decision at all.

That's where the Decision Matrix comes in. It's a simple but powerful tool that helps break down choices in a logical, structured way, so your decision isn't based on emotions or endless second-guessing but on clear priorities and real numbers.

It works like this: First, you write down all your options. Then, you choose the key factors that are most important in making your decision. These could be things like time, cost, personal satisfaction, long-term benefits, stress level—whatever matters most to you in this moment.

Once you have those factors, you rate each option on a scale of 1 to 5 based on how well it meets each criterion. After that, you total up the scores, and suddenly—there it is. The best choice isn't just a *feeling* anymore. It's right in front of you, laid out in a way that makes sense.

I remember using this when I was torn between two big opportunities. One option seemed like the "safe" choice—steady, predictable, no surprises. The other was more exciting but carried a lot of unknowns. I felt like I was stuck in a mental tug-of-war, unable to commit either way. But when I sat down and used the Decision Matrix, the answer became clear. Seeing it on paper instead of bouncing around in my head took away the emotional overwhelm. I wasn't relying on impulse—I had a logical reason for my decision.

That's what makes the Decision Matrix so effective. It helps you step out of the fog of indecision, remove the emotional guesswork, and prioritize what truly matters to you. Instead of feeling frozen by all the *what-ifs*, you finally have a clear path forward.

If you've been struggling to make a decision, I encourage you to try this. You might be surprised how much clarity comes from simply putting your choices into a structured system. Once you free yourself from the paralysis of indecision, you can move forward with confidence.

Medication and working with your Doctor

Before discussing ADHD medication in detail, it's important to note that I'm not a doctor and that this isn't medical advice. Everyone's journey with ADHD is unique, and what works for one person may not work for another. Medication is a personal choice, and the decision to pursue it should always be made in partnership with a trusted healthcare professional who understands your needs.

That said, if you decide to explore medication as part of your ADHD management, working closely with your doctor is essential. Open and honest communication about your symptoms—especially the specific challenges you face, like memory lapses, difficulty starting tasks, or feeling mentally scattered—helps your doctor determine the best approach for you. ADHD medications don't work the same way for everyone, and finding the right one often requires some trial and adjustment. It can take time to get the dosage or type of medication just right, and patience is key during this process. If something doesn't feel right—whether it's side effects, lack of effectiveness, or mood changes—letting your doctor know as soon as possible allows them to make the necessary adjustments.

Why does medication help? ADHD isn't just about distractions or forgetfulness—it's a neurological condition that affects how the brain regulates attention, motivation, and impulse control. Many people with ADHD have differences in how their brains process dopamine, a neurotransmitter responsible for focus and reward. When dopamine levels are too low or not efficiently transmitted, it can feel impossible to stay on track, follow through on tasks, or manage daily responsibilities.

Medication acts like a biochemical compass, helping to restore balance in the brain's neurotransmitter system. It doesn't *change* who you are and won't magically turn you into someone without ADHD, but it can clear the mental fog and make it easier to direct your focus where you want it to go. Instead of feeling like you're constantly fighting against your own brain, medication can provide the clarity, stability, and control needed to navigate daily life more effectively.

It's important to remember that medication isn't a standalone solution—it's one tool in a larger toolkit that can also include therapy, lifestyle changes, and personalized strategies for managing ADHD. Some people find that medication dramatically improves their quality of life, while others prefer to manage their symptoms through non-medication approaches. There's no "right" or "wrong" choice—just what works best for you.

If you're considering medication, the best thing you can do is approach the process with curiosity and self-awareness. Keep track of how you feel, what's working, and what isn't. Partner with a doctor who listens and is willing to fine-tune the approach as needed. Most importantly, give yourself grace. Finding what works takes time, and your journey with ADHD is uniquely yours to navigate.

Building Intentional Routines

The fog of ADHD can feel frustrating, disorienting, and even defeating at times. It's easy to fall into the trap of self-criticism, blaming yourself for things that feel out of control. But here's something I need you to hear: this fog is not a flaw—it's a symptom. It's not a reflection of your intelligence, effort, or worth. It's simply a challenge that comes with how your brain is wired. And like any challenge, it can be navigated with the right tools, support, and mindset.

One of the most powerful tools you can use is self-compassion. When you're lost in the fog, being kind to yourself is like having a compass that helps you find your way. Instead of getting stuck in cycles of frustration or shame, self-compassion allows you to acknowledge your struggles while still moving forward. It's about recognizing that progress isn't about perfection but persistence.

Think about the way you'd treat a friend who was struggling. If they came to you feeling overwhelmed and discouraged, you wouldn't tell them they were lazy or incapable. You'd remind them of their strengths, acknowledge their efforts, and encourage them to keep going. Now, imagine offering that same kindness to yourself. Instead of saying, *"I'm so disorganized"* or *"Why can't I just focus like everyone else?",* try reframing those thoughts with kindness: *"I'm figuring out what works for me"* or *"I may not have finished everything, but I showed up and tried today, and that matters."*

Self-compassion isn't about making excuses—it's about giving yourself the grace to grow. It takes practice, especially if you're used to being hard on yourself. But over time, treating yourself with kindness makes the fog feel less suffocating and more manageable.

Another key to navigating the fog is leaning on a support system. ADHD can make it hard to trust your own mental compass at times, but that's where the people around you come in. Think of your support system— whether it's family, friends, a therapist, or a mentor—as your iron rod, something steady to hold onto when the fog makes it difficult to see the path ahead. You don't have to navigate this alone.

Being open about your struggles is a powerful step in cutting through the fog. It's easy to keep things bottled up, thinking you need to figure everything out on your own. But when you say it out loud and share what you're going through with someone you trust, it lightens the weight of it. Talking about your challenges doesn't make them disappear but makes them feel less overwhelming and less impossible to manage.

If asking for help feels uncomfortable, start small. Be specific about what you need. Sometimes, ADHD fog makes it hard even to recognize the kind of support that would help most. Instead of saying, *"I'm struggling,"* try, *"Could you check in with me about my deadline next week?"* or *"Can we talk through some ideas? I feel stuck, and I need some outside perspective."* Small, clear requests make it easier for others to support you in ways that actually help.

Finding a community of people who understand ADHD can be a game-changer. There's something powerful about connecting with others who truly get it—who have experienced the same struggles and don't judge you for them. Whether it's an online ADHD community, a local support group, or even a close friend who shares similar challenges, surrounding yourself with people who "speak your language" can make a huge difference. It reminds you that you're not broken. You're not alone.

The truth is, the fog may come and go, but you are not powerless in it. With self-compassion, a solid support system, and intentional routines, you can create your own compass that helps you move forward, even when the path isn't always clear. The most important thing is to keep going. Even when progress feels slow, and the steps seem small, they are still steps forward. And that's what matters.

Leverage Technology

Let's face it: the ADHD brain sometimes struggles to hold onto important details, but the good news is that technology can act as an external brain—a reliable system that helps you stay organized and on track even when your internal compass feels a little off.

Use Digital Calendars: A simple calendar app like Google Calendar can be a game-changer. It allows you to schedule tasks, appointments, and reminders with time blocks to make your day more structured. You can also set up notifications to remind you when it's time to start something.

Task Management Apps: Apps like Todoist, Trello, or Motion allow you to organize tasks into categories, set deadlines, and prioritize what's most important. They're especially helpful when you're juggling multiple responsibilities and need to see everything in one place.

Voice Assistants: Tools like Siri, Alexa, or Google Assistant can help with on-the-spot reminders. For example, you can say, "Hey Siri, remind me to send that email at 2 p.m.," and you've offloaded one more thing from your mental load.

Timers and Alarms: Use timers to break tasks into manageable chunks, like 25 minutes of focused work followed by a 5-minute break.

(e.g., the Pomodoro Technique). This not only helps you get started but also keeps you focused on one task at a time without feeling overwhelmed.

The goal isn't to rely on technology to "fix" you but to use it as a tool to make your life easier. These apps and systems act like reliable compasses when you're navigating the fog, helping you focus on what matters most.

A Word of Encouragement

Navigating the fog isn't about getting it perfect. Some days, the fog will be thicker than others, and that's okay. The strategies we've talked about—self-compassion, support systems, and technology are tools, not cures. They won't magically clear the fog, but they'll help you take one step forward at a time.

And that's what matters. Every small step you take, every time you ask for help, every moment you treat yourself with kindness builds your path through the fog. You prove to yourself that you're capable, resourceful, and resilient.

So, as you move forward, remember this: the fog will come and go, but it's never permanent. With the right tools and support, you'll find your way through it. On the other side, there's a clearer, brighter version of the life you're building for yourself. You've got this!

Embracing the Compass

The fog of ADHD may feel disorienting, but it doesn't have to stop you. With tools like visual reminders, checklists, and routines, you can navigate even the thickest haze and find your way forward.

Remember, the fog is temporary. Each small step you take clears the path just a little more. With patience, compassion, and your compass, you'll move through the uncertainty and into clarity, one moment at a time.

"Remember: the whirlwind may be powerful, but so are you. With the right anchor, you can find stability, focus, and calm— even amid the storm."

Chapter 7

The Whirlwind and the Anchor

The Whirlwind of Overwhelm of Racing Thoughts can challenge even the best of us. Imagine standing in the middle of a whirlwind. Papers are flying, objects are tumbling, and the noise is overwhelming. You're trying to grab onto something, anything, to stop the chaos, but it all feels out of reach. For us with ADHD, this is often what your mental and physical energy feels like. A whirlwind of thoughts, tasks, and distractions pulling you in every direction at once.

What Does the Whirlwind Look Like?

The whirlwind is a hallmark symptom of ADHD. driven by the brain's constant search for stimulation and its difficulty with prioritization and organization. The whirlwind of ADHD can manifest in many ways. You might:

Start Multiple Tasks: You begin folding laundry and then notice your inbox is full. You start responding to emails and then scroll through social media, leaving everything half-finished.

Feel Mentally Overloaded: Thoughts race through your mind at lightning speed, making it hard to focus on one thing.

Struggle to Prioritize: Everything feels equally urgent, leading to either frantic multitasking or freezing up completely.

Picture this, you wake up determined to have a productive day. You start cleaning the kitchen, but midway through, you remember you need to reply to an email. While typing your reply, you notice a bill that needs paying, so you open your banking app—but before you finish, a notification on your phone grabs your attention. By the end of the day, you feel exhausted but can't point to anything you've truly accomplished. That's the whirlwind in action.

The Anchor: Grounding Yourself Amidst Chaos

Life with ADHD can often feel like being caught in a storm—thoughts racing in all directions, emotions shifting rapidly, and focus slipping away before you even realize it. It's exhausting, frustrating, and, at times, completely overwhelming. But just like a ship navigating turbulent waters, you don't have to be at the mercy of the storm. An anchor doesn't stop the waves, but it keeps the ship from being swept away. That's exactly what grounding techniques do for the ADHD mind. They don't eliminate the chaos entirely, but they provide a steady point of stability—something you can return to when everything feels like it's moving too fast.

Grounding yourself in moments of being overwhelmed is about regaining control, finding your center, and giving yourself the space to reset. One of the simplest and most effective ways to do this is deep breathing. It might sound too simple, but there's real science behind it. When stress, anxiety, or mental overload takes over, your nervous system shifts into high alert, making it even harder to focus or think clearly. Deep breathing signals to your brain that you are safe, activating the body's relaxation response and helping to slow everything down.

Breathing is something we do automatically, but intentional breathing can be a powerful tool. Instead of getting lost in a whirlwind of thoughts, shifting your attention to your breath pulls you back into the present moment. It's like grabbing hold of that anchor—something solid to focus on while everything else settles.

One technique that works well is box breathing. Imagine drawing a square in your mind as you breathe. Inhale deeply for four counts, hold your breath for four counts, exhale slowly for four counts, and then pause for another four counts before repeating the cycle. This creates a rhythm, a structure for your breath to follow, which helps bring a sense of order to the chaos inside your mind. The best part? You can do it anytime, anywhere—whether you're in the middle of a stressful situation or just need a moment to reset.

Another method, diaphragmatic breathing, focuses on engaging the full depth of your breath. Instead of shallow chest breathing, which can make stress feel even more intense, this technique encourages deep belly breathing that calms the nervous system. Place one hand on your chest and the other on your abdomen. As you take a slow, deep breath in, feel your belly rise while your chest stays relatively still. Then, exhale fully, letting your abdomen fall naturally. This type of breathing activates the parasympathetic nervous system, signaling to your body that it's okay to relax.

Deep breathing might seem small, but its impact is significant. It shifts your focus away from the mental chaos and back to something steady, predictable, and calming—your breath. When you give yourself a moment to breathe, to pause, and to reset, you create the space you need to regain control, refocus, and move forward with clarity. The storm may still be there, but with your anchor in place, you won't be lost in it.

The whirlwind thrives on a lack of structure. Prioritization exercises provide clarity by breaking down competing tasks and identifying what truly matters. The Eisenhower Matrix is a great tool for prioritizing tasks.

The Eisenhower Matrix: Divide tasks into four categories:

Urgent and important	Important but not urgent
1. 2. 3.	1. 2. 3.
Urgent but not important	Neither urgent nor important
1. 2. 3.	1. 2. 3.

4. **Urgent and Important:** Do these first.

5. **Important but Not Urgent:** Schedule these for later.

6. **Urgent but Not Important:** Delegate these if possible.

7. **Neither Urgent nor Important:** Eliminate or postpone these.

Task Triaging: Start by listing all the tasks swirling in your mind. Then, Group similar tasks together to reduce mental clutter. Finally, choose one "anchor task" for the day (a single priority that anchors your focus and provides a sense of accomplishment).

Note: Prioritization reduces the overwhelming sense of "everything at once " by creating a clear plan of action, giving you a manageable path forward.

Self-Reflection: Gaining Perspective on the Storm

When you're caught in the whirlwind of ADHD—thoughts racing, emotions running high, tasks piling up—it's easy to feel like you're just reacting to life instead of living it with intention. Everything feels urgent and important, and before you know it, the day is gone, and you're left wondering what even happened. This constant mental storm can make it difficult to see the bigger picture, to step back and understand why you feel overwhelmed, scattered, or stuck.

That's where **self-reflection** comes in. It's not about overanalyzing every detail of your life or criticizing yourself for what went wrong—it's about pausing long enough to gain clarity, to recognize patterns, and to give yourself the chance to make intentional choices instead of being swept away by the chaos. When you take even a few moments to reflect, you create space between yourself and the storm, allowing you to respond with awareness rather than impulsive reaction.

One of the simplest ways to do this is through **journaling**. You don't have to be a writer, and you don't need to worry about making it sound good. The point isn't to craft a perfect entry—it's to get your thoughts out of your head and onto paper where you can see them more clearly. Set a five or ten-minute timer, and write about what's on your mind. What's causing stress? What emotions are surfacing? What's been weighing on you? As you start to put words to your thoughts, you might notice patterns—certain triggers that consistently throw you off, recurring frustrations, or even small victories that deserve more recognition. Writing things down helps you process emotions in a way that thinking alone often can't. It turns vague feelings into something tangible, something you can work with.

Another simple yet powerful practice is an **end-of-day check-in**. ADHD often makes time feel slippery—days blur together, making it hard to track what's working and what isn't. Taking a moment at the end of the day to reflect helps bring awareness to how you're moving through life. Ask yourself: What went well today? Perhaps you finished a task that had been hanging over your head, or maybe you managed a tough situation better than you expected. Then, consider: What could I improve tomorrow? Not in a self-critical way, but as an opportunity to learn. Maybe you noticed that checking your phone first thing in the morning threw off your focus or that skipping lunch made it harder to concentrate in the afternoon. Finally, ask yourself: What do I need to let go of? Some days don't go as planned, and that's okay. Holding onto frustration, guilt, or perfectionism only makes it harder to move forward. Letting go of what didn't work allows you to start fresh the next day with a clearer mind.

Self-reflection works because it gives you perspective on your own life. It helps you separate yourself from the whirlwind rather than being consumed by it. It reminds you that ADHD doesn't define you—it's just a part of your story. And when you take the time to check in with yourself, even in small ways, you create an opportunity to move through life with greater awareness, intention, and self-compassion.

Mindfulness Practices: Staying Present Amidst Racing Thoughts

For an ADHD mind, staying present can feel like trying to hold onto water, slipping through your fingers no matter how hard you try. Thoughts race ahead, worries multiply, and your brain constantly pulls you toward the next thing, making it difficult to focus on what's right in front of you. The whirlwind of mental noise can be exhausting, leaving you feeling scattered, anxious, and unable to fully engage with the moment you're in.

That's where mindfulness comes in. It's not about forcing yourself to "clear your mind" or eliminating distractions altogether. Instead, it's about learning to observe your thoughts without getting lost in them, like watching clouds drift across the sky rather than being caught in a storm. Mindfulness helps create space between you and the chaos, grounding you in the present moment so you can move through life with greater clarity and calm.

Five Senses Grounding Exercise Is One simple but powerful way to do this. When your thoughts feel overwhelming, this technique brings you out of your head and back into your body, reconnecting you to your surroundings. Start by noticing five things you can see—the color of the sky, the pattern of light on the walls, and the shape of your hands. Then, shift your attention to four things you can touch—the fabric of your clothing, the smooth surface of a table, and the weight of your feet against the floor. Next, listen for three things you can hear—the hum of an appliance, distant voices, your own breath. Then move to two things you can smell—maybe the scent of Pine trees, fresh air, or even the absence of a strong smell. Finally, focus on one thing you can taste, whether it's a sip of water, a piece of gum, or just the lingering flavor of your last meal. This exercise grounds you in your senses, gently pulling your awareness away from racing thoughts and into the reality of the present moment.

Self-Awareness Scan: Another way to cultivate mindfulness is through a, which helps you reconnect with your body and recognize where you're holding tension or emotions. Close your eyes and take a slow, deep breath. Begin by focusing on the top of your head and mentally scan downward, noticing any areas of tightness, discomfort, or sensation. Pay attention to where you physically feel your stress—is there tightness in your shoulders, a clenching in your jaw, or restlessness in your hands? You don't have to change anything or force yourself to relax—just observe. By doing this, you begin to understand how emotions show up in your body, giving you the awareness to release tension before it builds up into being overwhelming.

Mindfulness works because it shifts attention from abstract thoughts to tangible experiences, creating a sense of stability in the present moment. Instead of being carried away by racing thoughts or overwhelming worries, you can anchor yourself, reset, and regain control. It's a practice, not a perfect solution, but the more you practice it, the easier it becomes to find clarity even in the midst of mental chaos.

Building a Physical Anchor

ADHD often feels like living in motion—thoughts racing, tasks piling up, and a constant sense that you're being pulled in a hundred different directions at once. It's easy to feel overwhelmed, especially when your physical environment mirrors that same chaos. A cluttered space can exacerbate mental clutter, making it even harder to focus and find clarity. When everything around you feels out of place, your mind follows suit—jumping from one unfinished task to another, unable to settle.

That's why creating a physical anchor is so powerful. Just as grounding techniques help calm your thoughts, an intentional, organized space can provide a sense of stability and control amidst the whirlwind. It's not about creating a perfectly minimalist home or having color-coded shelves for everything you own—it's about designing an environment that supports your focus rather than fighting against it. When your surroundings are set up to work with you, they become a tool for clarity rather than another source of distraction.

Decluttering your space: one of the simplest ways to eliminate distractions. I'll be honest—this hasn't always come naturally to me. I used to tell myself that my messy desk was just part of my "creative process," but deep down, I knew that the clutter made it harder to start tasks, stay focused, and follow through on what mattered most. Every time I sat down to work, my brain had to fight through the visual noise before I could even begin. The issue wasn't just the physical mess—it was the mental drain of constantly being reminded of unfinished tasks and misplaced items.

What ultimately helped was realizing that I didn't need to organize everything all at once. Instead, I started small. One drawer. One surface. One section of my workspace. Each time I cleared unnecessary clutter, I felt more mentally clear and in control. I also began using storage solutions that truly worked for me—clear bins so I could see what I needed at a glance, labeled folders to keep important papers from going missing, and small trays to hold frequently used items so they didn't end up scattered across my desk. The difference was immediate. I no longer had to waste time looking for things, and my space felt less overwhelming, making it easier to focus.

Visual cues: Another helpful strategy to stay grounded. My brain is naturally forgetful, so relying on memory alone is a losing battle. Instead of constantly feeling like I have to "keep track of everything," I've learned to offload reminders into my environment. Simple things—like keeping a to-do list in plain sight, using sticky notes with key priorities, or even placing a motivational quote where I'll see it first thing in the morning—act as anchors that bring my attention back to what matters. I also use color-coded systems to organize tasks—certain colors for urgent deadlines, different colors for long-term projects—so I can see at a glance what needs attention without feeling overwhelmed.

Even with an organized space, there are still moments when my mind feels like it's spinning out of control. That's when immediate grounding techniques become essential. These techniques help interrupt the mental whirlwind, allowing me to reset and regain control before I spiral further.

One of my favorite techniques is the **5-4-3-2-1 grounding exercise**. There have been many times when my thoughts felt so scattered that I couldn't even figure out where to begin. But instead of forcing myself to "just focus," I take a moment to pause and reconnect with my senses. I look around and name **five things I can see**—the texture of my desk, the color of the walls, and the pattern of light on the floor. Next, I focus on **four things I can touch**—the fabric of my shirt, the texture of my Leather journal, and the cool surface of my laptop. I listen for **three things I can hear**: the hum of the air conditioner, distant traffic, or the faint clicking of my keyboard. I shift my attention to **two things I can smell**, like the scent of pine trees or the fresh air coming through the window. Finally, I notice **one thing I can taste**—even if it's just the lingering flavor of my last sip of water. By the time I finish this exercise, my brain feels calmer, more settled, and more present. Instead of getting lost in mental chaos, I'm back in my body, grounded in the moment.

Deep breathing: Another simple but powerful grounding tool is when my mind is racing, my body follows—I tense up, my breathing gets shallow, and I start feeling more anxious. We've talked about Deep Breathing earlier in the book, but it's a technique that will span through all the elements of the storm. Slowing down your breath signals to your nervous system that it's okay to relax. Inhale deeply for four seconds, hold it for four seconds, then exhale for four seconds, repeating the cycle until you feel your body start to release the tension. Sometimes, I'll pair this with **physical grounding**—placing your feet flat on the floor, pressing down firmly, and feeling the connection to the ground beneath you. There's something about physically reminding yourself that you exist, that you are stable, and that you are okay, which helps calm the storm inside your mind.

These grounding techniques don't eliminate the whirlwind entirely, but they provide enough stillness to navigate it with greater clarity and purpose. Whether you're organizing your space, using visual cues, or practicing sensory grounding exercises, each tool helps ground you in the present moment instead of getting lost in the storm. ADHD brings a lot of energy, movement, and unpredictability—but with the right anchors in place, that energy can be directed rather than scattered and harnessed instead of overwhelming. It's not about stopping the whirlwind; it's about learning how to move through it with stability, confidence, and focus.

Channeling the Whirlwind: Chaos into Creativity

ADHD energy is often likened to a **whirlwind**, a continuous storm of thoughts, ideas, and impulses, pulling in various directions. It can feel overwhelming—like no matter how hard you strive to get organized, your brain is always two steps ahead, throwing out new ideas before you've even finished processing the last one. But here's something I've learned: the whirlwind isn't merely a challenge—it's also a source of immense creative potential. The same mental energy that makes focus difficult is also what enables ADHD minds to think outside the box, generate fresh ideas, and find solutions that others might overlook. The key isn't to try to suppress the whirlwind—it's to channel it into something productive.

For a long time, I fought against my natural mental energy, believing that if I could just be more "disciplined," I could somehow compel myself to work in a manner that felt more structured and linear. However, that never succeeded because it contradicted how my brain is wired. What ultimately made the difference was learning to harness the energy of the whirlwind instead of resisting it.

Instead of forcing myself into rigid structures that didn't fit, I began to harness **bursts of mental energy** to my advantage. When I experienced a surge of focus and creativity, I leaned into it—utilizing those moments for brainstorming, problem-solving, or deep creative work. However, I recognized that if I didn't establish some boundaries, that same spontaneity could leave me scattered, with half-finished projects and no clear direction. So, I created structured flexibility—I allotted dedicated time for unstructured exploration, allowing me to pursue creative impulses without guilt but within limits to prevent completely losing track of my priorities. This approach enabled me to capture the excitement of the moment without letting it derail everything else.

One of the biggest shifts for me was learning to **capture ideas** as they come instead of allowing them to pile up in my head. ADHD often brings rapid-fire thoughts, and if I don't write them down, they either disappear completely or create mental clutter that makes it difficult to concentrate. I started keeping a notebook and a digital app close at hand —something simple, nothing complicated—so I could quickly jot down ideas, to-do list items, or random thoughts as they arose. This small habit made a significant difference because it allowed me to transfer ideas from my mind to paper, where I could revisit them later without feeling like I was losing something important in the chaos. It was a game-changer for managing my creative energy without becoming overwhelmed by it.

Prioritization: Choosing What Matters Most

Even with better systems in place, there was still one challenge I couldn't ignore: when everything feels equally important, nothing gets done. ADHD makes it difficult to filter out what actually matters, and when you're staring at an endless list of tasks, it's easy to either shut down completely or jump between tasks without making real progress. Learning to prioritize effectively was the turning point for me.

I used to start my day feeling like I had a *"HUNDRED"* things I needed to do, but instead of working through them in a way that made sense, I'd end up doing bits and pieces of different tasks without finishing anything. That left me feeling frustrated, unproductive, and constantly behind.

What helped was a simple but powerful shift: choosing the **Top Three tasks** for the day.

At the start of each morning, I take a few moments to decide on the three most important things I need to get done—not everything I *want* to do, not everything that's buzzing in my mind, but the three things that will have the biggest impact. I write them down and commit to focusing on them first before getting caught up in distractions. This small habit has been life-changing because it cuts through the noise, giving my brain clear direction instead of letting me get lost in an overwhelming to-do list. I can still do other tasks if time allows, but having a clear priority list ensures that even on my most scattered days, I make progress where it matters most.

When I have multiple projects going at once, I sometimes use a system called the **Eisenhower Matrix** to help me decide what to tackle first. Before, I used to treat every task as equally urgent, but I realized that wasn't true-some tasks were time-sensitive, while others felt urgent in the moment but weren't actually important. The Eisenhower Matrix helped me sort tasks into four categories:

1. **Urgent and important** – These need immediate attention, like meeting a deadline or handling a pressing issue.
2. **Important but not urgent:** These tasks contribute to long-term goals but don't have immediate deadlines, such as skill-building or deep work on a personal project.
3. **Urgent but not important** – These often feel pressing but don't necessarily require my focus, like responding to non-critical emails.
4. **Neither urgent nor important** – These can be delegated, postponed, or removed entirely.

When I started visually categorizing my tasks, I realized just how often I was prioritizing things that *felt* urgent but weren't actually the most important. Using this method helped me take control of my time and focus my energy on what actually moved me forward instead of getting stuck in reactive mode.

Time-blocking also made a big difference in helping me stay on track. My ADHD brain tends to jump from one thing to another, and without some structure, I'd spend all day working without feeling like I'd actually accomplished anything. When I started setting specific times for different types of tasks, everything changed. Instead of checking emails randomly throughout the day, I dedicated an hour in the morning to clear my inbox. Instead of bouncing between work projects, I set aside focused time for deep work. This approach created mental boundaries that helped me stay engaged with one task at a time rather than getting lost in multitasking.

I remember a time when I had several projects piling up, and I felt completely paralyzed by indecision. I had no idea where to start, so I ended up wasting time on small, unimportant tasks just to feel like I was doing *something*. When I finally sat down and set aside time for each project, everything fell into place. Instead of spinning my wheels, I had a clear plan, dedicated time, and a sense of control over my schedule. It didn't make my ADHD disappear, but it provided a structure that worked *with* my brain instead of against it.

At the end of the day, prioritization isn't about doing everything—it's about doing the right things. ADHD thrives on novelty and urgency, but not everything is equally important. Once I learned to cut through the chaos and focus my energy on what truly mattered, I felt less overwhelmed, more productive, and more in control of my time. The whirlwind still exists, but now I know how to channel it into meaningful work instead of allowing it to scatter my focus.

Creating Systems for Stability

One of the biggest challenges of ADHD is that everything can feel unpredictable—some days, you're focused and productive, while other days, even the simplest tasks seem impossible to start. That inconsistency can be exhausting. It's like trying to build on shifting sand—without a stable foundation, everything feels fragile and uncertain.

That's where systems come into play. Having structure doesn't mean stifling your natural energy or creativity. In fact, the right systems do the opposite—they establish a solid framework that provides stability while still allowing for flexibility. Systems help you continue progressing even on days when motivation is lacking. They alleviate the mental burden, making it easier to stay on track without constantly relying on willpower alone.

One of the best ways to create stability is by establishing routines for repetitive tasks. ADHD thrives on novelty, which can make routine feel boring at times, but having default systems for everyday tasks can reduce decision fatigue and prevent small obstacles from piling up. I used to struggle with starting my mornings in an organized way—some days, I'd jump straight into work, while other days, I'd scroll on my phone for an hour, and before I knew it, half the morning was gone. What finally helped was creating a morning routine checklist—nothing rigid, just a simple structure to help me start the day in a way that set me up for success. Instead of guessing what I should do first, I had a sequence to follow, such as brushing my teeth, reviewing my calendar, and writing down my top three priorities for the day. It wasn't about being perfect—it was about making mornings feel less chaotic and more intentional.

Another system that made a huge difference was using checklists for bigger projects. ADHD brains love big ideas but struggle with breaking them down into actionable steps. I used to write vague to-do lists that would sit untouched for weeks because they were overwhelming. Instead of writing something broad like *"Plan vacation,"* I learned to break it down into manageable steps: *"Book flights," "Choose hotel,"* and *"Create packing list."* Suddenly, tasks that once felt massive became manageable steps I could actually follow through on.

I also discovered that having an accountability partner made a significant difference. ADHD can make it easy to set goals, but also make it difficult to stick to them or lose momentum halfway through. When I began sharing my priorities with a trusted friend, it became much easier to remain on track. Knowing that someone else would check in on my progress provided me with an extra layer of accountability that my brain needed. It wasn't about pressure or guilt—it was about establishing a support system that helped me maintain focus.

I remember a time when I struggled to keep up with everything in my business. I had deadlines, projects, and emails to respond to, but my mind kept jumping between tasks, making it impossible to complete anything. I began each workday by writing a checklist for the next morning. Then, I'd text my goals to a friend, not because they needed to hold me accountable, but because saying them out loud made them feel more real. These simple systems provided me with a sense of control, helping me feel grounded instead of overwhelmed.

Having these structures in place doesn't guarantee that every day will be perfectly productive. However, it means that on tough days, when my mind feels scattered and unfocused, I have something to rely on. I don't have to start from scratch each morning. I don't need to waste energy deciding *what* to do—I already have a system that supports me.

Mindful Pauses: Slowing Down to Speed Up

When you have ADHD, it's easy to feel like you need to keep pushing forward—that if you just work harder, stay up later, or power through exhaustion, you'll finally get everything done. The problem is that this approach usually leads straight to burnout. What I didn't realize for years was that slowing down doesn't make you less productive; in fact, it helps you work smarter, with more clarity and efficiency.

Mindful pauses create space to reset your mind, preventing the type of mental exhaustion that makes it harder to concentrate. Initially, I resisted taking breaks because I believed I didn't have *time* for them. However, I quickly learned that burning myself out ultimately made me less productive in the long run.

One of the easiest ways I began to incorporate pauses into my day was by setting alarms to remind me to take short breaks. I often hyper-focus on tasks, which means I can go for hours without moving, drinking water, or even realizing how much time has passed. Setting a timer to take a five-minute break every hour helped me reset without completely losing momentum. I would stand up, stretch, and drink some water—just enough to refresh my brain before diving back into work with renewed energy.

Another game-changer was taking a few minutes at the end of the day to **reflect and reset**. ADHD makes time feel slippery—days blur together, and it's easy to feel like you're constantly working but never making real progress. Instead of going to bed with my mind racing about what I *didn't* get done, I started asking myself three simple questions: *What went well today? What can I improve tomorrow? What do I need to let go of?* This practice helped me **acknowledge small wins**, adjust my approach without guilt, and mentally close the chapter on the day so I wasn't carrying unfinished thoughts into the next morning.

Celebrating small wins was one of the hardest things for me to learn. ADHD often makes you focus on what's unfinished instead of what you've already accomplished. I used to end my days feeling like I had barely made a dent in my to-do list, even when I had actually done a lot. When I started intentionally pausing to recognize progress—whether it was finishing a project, making an important call, or even just sticking to my routine—I noticed a huge shift in my mindset. Instead of constantly feeling like I was behind, I started feeling motivated to keep going.

When I first started using these pauses, I worried they would slow me down. But they had the opposite effect—they made me more efficient, focused, and less mentally exhausted. Instead of running on empty and crashing at the end of the day, I could pace myself, work more effectively, and still have energy for the things that mattered outside of work.

Mindful pauses aren't just about doing *less;* they're about working in a way that genuinely supports your brain instead of exhausting it. ADHD can make you feel like you always need to be in motion, constantly chasing the next thing. However, taking intentional breaks creates a rhythm that makes your work more sustainable, sharpens your focus, and stabilizes your energy.

At the end of the day, creating systems for stability and allowing yourself moments of pause are fundamentally similar: they make life easier for your ADHD brain, rather than constantly fighting against it. The more you collaborate *with* yourself rather than against yourself, the more you'll discover a sense of clarity, balance, and control in the whirlwind. The cost of an Untamed Whirlwind.

The whirlwind can be exhausting, both mentally and emotionally. It often leads to feeling overwhelmed and can result in procrastination or avoidance, causing missed deadlines or abandoned projects. The constant activity in your mind makes it hard to think clearly, leading to stress and frustration. With so many things started but not finished, it can feel like you're spinning your wheels without making progress. The chaos can leave you feeling defeated, questioning why you can't just "get it together." These racing thoughts often worsen anxiety or frustration, making it harder to face challenges effectively. The ongoing mental chaos makes it difficult to complete tasks, resulting in missed deadlines and increased stress. This relentless turbulence of racing thoughts and being overwhelmed can lead to forgetfulness, missed commitments, or impulsive reactions, straining personal connections at home and in the workplace. Frequently feeling unable to manage the whirlwind can lead to guilt, shame, and a sense of failure. That shame and constant mental noise drain emotional and physical energy, contributing to burnout.

But here's the grand truth: the whirlwind isn't a failure; it's a natural part of how the ADHD brain works. And just like any storm, it can be navigated. The key is finding your anchor— a tool or practice that helps you regain stability and focus.

Embracing the Anchor

The whirlwind of ADHD is not something to fight against—it's a natural part of who you are. But with tools like grounding techniques, prioritization, and mindful pauses, you can anchor yourself amidst the chaos and harness your energy in meaningful ways. View the whirlwind not as a hindrance but as a dynamic force that, when grounded, can propel you forward.

Remember: the whirlwind may be powerful, but so are you. With the right anchor, you can find stability, focus, and calm, even amid the storm.

"Your shelter isn't about escaping the storm; it's about creating a space where you can recharge and step back into the world stronger than before."

CHAPTER 8

The Shelter and Building a Safe Haven

Without it, you are exposed to feelings of vulnerability and burnout. Living with ADHD often means facing heightened stress, overwhelming emotions, and the exhaustion of constantly managing symptoms. Many individuals with ADHD experience periods of burnout, where even small tasks feel insurmountable, or moments when they feel overly exposed to criticism, failure, or judgment from others.

So, creating a personal support system and self-care practices serves as a shelter from life's storms. The shelter represents a protective, restorative space where individuals can recharge, practice self-compassion, and regain strength. This "safe haven" might include cultivating a supportive community, setting up physical spaces for peace, or developing routines that help manage overwhelm.

The overall objective is to explore ways to create emotional, physical, and social "shelters" that protect against burnout and reinforce resilience. This chapter will provide tools for building supportive relationships, practicing restorative self-care, setting healthy boundaries, and creating environments (both physical and emotional) that feel safe and nurturing.

A Place of Safety and Stability

Imagine being caught in a storm—rain pouring down, wind howling, and no end in sight. Then, just as the chaos feels overwhelming, you spot a small shelter in the distance. You step inside, and suddenly, you're dry, warm, and safe. This is what a shelter represents for individuals with ADHD: a space of comfort, stability, and security amidst the storms of life.

The world for someone with ADHD can feel loud, overwhelming, and relentless. Constant distractions, heightened emotions, and the daily challenges of managing tasks can make it hard to feel grounded. A shelter isn't about escaping from these challenges—it's about creating spaces and systems that allow you to thrive despite them. It's a foundation of safety and support that gives you the strength to face the storms.

You might be wondering, "Why do I need a shelter?" And you know what? I had the same thought at first! So, let's take a moment to dive into what ADHD is all about and why setting up a shelter or a solid strategy can really make a difference. Having a shelter is essential for navigating the unique challenges that come with ADHD. You can easily feel scattered, overwhelmed, or emotionally drained without it. A well-designed shelter can help you manage all that and provide:

A Recharge Point: A place to retreat and replenish your energy after a busy or overwhelming day.

A Sense of Control: A stable foundation that helps you regain focus when chaos threatens to take over.

A Comfort Zone: Emotional and physical security that allows you to face challenges with confidence.

The ever-present vulnerability and burnout that often accompany ADHD can be debilitating and overwhelming, leading to excessive stress. Even periods of high energy can result in exhaustion if not managed properly. Given that these emotional states are consistently present, it becomes essential to learn how to recognize the signs of burnout before it reaches a critical point.

To give yourself a starting advantage, it's important to develop a personal support system. The value of a trusted support network—friends, family, mentors, or support groups—lies in its ability to offer guidance and connection. For example, finding ADHD-friendly communities in person or online allows you to connect with others who understand and relate to your experiences. In these spaces, you can foster relationships based on understanding and encouragement and create a critical "shelter" against criticism and judgment. Additionally, consider creating physical spaces for restoration by setting up calming, organized environments in your home or workplace where you can decompress. A clutter-free, soothing space minimizes sensory distractions, and designing a "sanctuary" at home provides a retreat when life feels overwhelming, contributing to building your shelter. This sanctuary is where you can begin to practice self-compassion and challenge negative self-talk, forming a foundation for your shelter that bolsters your confidence to continue building. Of course, we shouldn't neglect self-care routines that nurture our mental and emotional well-being, such as nutrition, rest, journaling, meditation, and creative expression. Believe it or not, these are important parts of your shelter. We will learn to incorporate "shelter moments" into our day, taking short breaks to recharge emotionally and mentally.

Boundaries as part of your shelter

Establishing healthy boundaries in personal and professional relationships serves as a "shelter" that prevents being overwhelmed and protects one's energy. We will explore practical tips for communicating boundaries clearly and assertively without guilt. It is crucial to "protect" one's time and mental well-being by declining commitments or demands that do not align with personal goals or needs.

Your shelter should provide routines and rituals that reinforce the shelter: daily practices that foster a sense of stability and safety. For example, grounding exercises, evening wind-down routines, or weekly self-care check-ins can help you stay connected to yourself. Understand how rituals can bring familiarity and calm, strengthening the shelter even in challenging times. As you build your shelter, remember that it is ever-changing, and you must strengthen and maintain it by periodically checking in on your emotional, physical, and social needs. This is often achieved with reflection questions to identify areas in your life where you may feel unprotected or in need of extra care. Just as any shelter requires upkeep, your self-care and support need continuous attention to remain strong and effective.

Physiology of ADHD: The Need for a "Shelter"

ADHD is not merely a collection of behavioral traits; it has a specific physiological foundation rooted in brain structure, neurochemistry, and how the body processes stress and sensory input. Understanding these physiological factors clarifies why individuals with ADHD often experience a heightened need for safe, calm environments—a refuge from the sensory and emotional intensity of daily life. Let's examine the different aspects of physiology more closely.

Dopamine Regulation: Protection from the Storm.

Dopamine is a small molecule that plays a significant role in how your brain functions. It acts as a neurotransmitter—a chemical messenger that relays signals between different brain regions, influencing motivation, pleasure, and emotional regulation. Think of it as the brain's reward messenger, responsible for that satisfying sense of accomplishment when you complete a task or achieve a goal. It makes certain activities feel engaging, fuels curiosity, and reinforces habits that bring a sense of fulfillment. However, with ADHD, this system doesn't operate in quite the same way. The brain's dopamine pathways function differently, leading to inconsistent motivation, difficulties with sustained focus, and a continual search for stimulation. This difference impacts nearly every aspect of life —productivity, decision-making, emotional regulation, and even the ability to follow through on important tasks that lack immediate satisfaction. When dopamine levels are low or inefficiently transmitted, staying engaged with routine tasks can feel nearly impossible, while exciting or novel activities capture full attention effortlessly. Understanding this difference is essential for working with your brain rather than against it, finding strategies that support focus and motivation, and building systems that make success more sustainable. Let's break it down:

Lower Baseline Dopamine Levels: Research shows that people with ADHD often have lower levels of dopamine in key areas of the brain, particularly the prefrontal cortex. This part of the brain governs executive functions like focus, planning, and impulse control. When dopamine is low, it's like running a car on fumes—you can function, but everything feels harder, slower, and less efficient.

Inefficient Dopamine Transport: Even when dopamine is present, the ADHD brain often struggles to process and transport it effectively. This means that the signals responsible for maintaining focus, regulating emotions, or finishing tasks don't get where they need to go as smoothly as they should.

Dopamine Craving and Stimulation: Because the brain is always searching for that dopamine boost, individuals with ADHD often feel drawn to activities that promise quick rewards. This might be scrolling through social media, starting a new project, or diving into something exciting—but it can also mean difficulty staying engaged in routine or low-stimulation tasks, like paying bills or folding laundry.

The Consequences of Dopamine Dysregulation

This unique relationship with dopamine can create a fascinating and frustrating cycle: To compensate for low dopamine, the brain seeks out activities that feel rewarding. This can lead to impulsive decisions, hyperfocus on exciting tasks, or a tendency to procrastinate on things that do not provide immediate satisfaction.

While chasing dopamine, it's easy to become overstimulated—there is too much sensory input, too many tasks, or too many emotional highs and lows. Over time, this can lead to burnout, leaving one feeling drained, unfocused, and emotionally exhausted.

The ADHD brain frequently finds it difficult to sustain motivation for long-term goals or repetitive tasks. This isn't laziness; rather, it stems from the brain's wiring, which favors immediate rewards over delayed gratification.

The Role of the Shelter in Dopamine Regulation

Now, let's discuss how the Shelter connects to this. When you envision the Shelter, think of it as a space, both physical and mental, that serves as a buffer between you and the overwhelming stimulation of the world. For someone with ADHD, a well-designed Shelter is essential because it offers a controlled environment where dopamine levels can stabilize.

When you're overstimulated, your brain faces a barrage of dopamine-triggering inputs—noises, visuals, choices, and distractions. Even seemingly minor things, like a loud TV or a messy desk, can contribute to the chaos. A Shelter reduces this sensory overload by fostering a calm, organized environment.

Consider quiet corners, soft lighting, calming colors, and uncluttered surfaces. These elements help minimize the urge for constant dopamine-chasing activities, allowing your brain the space it needs to relax. Your brain requires downtime to recover from the fluctuations of dopamine spikes. The Shelter offers a restorative environment where your brain can reset.

In a quiet environment with fewer distractions and demands, your brain doesn't constantly seek the next dopamine rush. This allows dopamine levels to stabilize naturally, decreasing feelings of being overwhelmed or burned out.

Remember, a shelter doesn't eliminate all stimulation—it provides intentional, balanced stimulation. For example:

Mindful Activities: Activities like journaling, meditation, or painting provide gentle dopamine boosts without overwhelming your brain.

Physical Movement: Exercise is one of the best ways to boost dopamine naturally. A Shelter might include space for yoga, stretching, or even dancing to your favorite music.

Small Rewards: Incorporating small, manageable rewards into your day can provide controlled dopamine hits. For example, you can enjoy a favorite snack after completing a task or take a short walk after a work session.

The Shelter as a Long-Term Solution

Understanding dopamine regulation isn't just about avoiding burnout— it's about creating a sustainable rhythm for your brain, a way to work *with* your natural tendencies instead of constantly battling against them. When you have ADHD, managing focus, motivation, and emotional balance isn't just a matter of willpower—it's about building an environment and routines that actively support your brain's needs. This is where the concept of The Shelter comes in—a physical and mental space where you can reclaim focus, build resilience, and celebrate small wins in a way that reinforces healthy dopamine cycles.

Reclaiming focus starts with removing distractions and reducing sensory overload. ADHD brains are naturally wired to seek stimulation, which means that an overstimulating environment can make it nearly impossible to concentrate. Creating a Shelter means setting up a space that filters out distractions and helps your brain stay engaged with what matters. This doesn't mean you need a silent, empty room—just an area where you feel mentally clear, physically comfortable, and free from constant interruptions. A low-stimulation zone might be a quiet corner with minimal clutter, soft lighting, and a comfortable chair—somewhere you can go when you need to focus without feeling overwhelmed by everything around you.

Building resilience happens when you reinforce healthy dopamine cycles. The Shelter isn't just a place to work—it's also a space to reset and recharge so that your brain doesn't constantly run on empty. When you consistently give yourself time to step away, regulate emotions, and recover from overstimulation, you make it easier to handle challenges without completely burning out. This means designing routines that alternate between periods of deep focus and intentional rest, so you're not stuck in an all-or-nothing cycle of hyper-focus followed by exhaustion. Working on a high-focus task for 25 minutes, then taking five minutes to stretch, breathe, or step outside, creates a rhythm that keeps energy levels steady instead of crashing.

Celebrating small wins is crucial because dopamine thrives on reinforcement. The Shelter becomes a space where you acknowledge and reward progress, even when it feels small. Instead of only recognizing major accomplishments, take time to celebrate moments like finishing a difficult email, making progress on a project, or simply staying on task for longer than usual. The more you intentionally recognize these wins, the more you reinforce positive behaviors and motivation. Keeping a visual reminder of your achievements—like a checklist, a habit tracker, or even a small notebook where you jot down completed tasks—can help retrain your brain to see progress instead of focusing only on what's left undone.

Setting Up Your Shelter

Setting up a Shelter that actively supports dopamine regulation starts with designing a space that balances stimulation. Too much stimulation can lead to distraction, but too little can make tasks feel impossible to start. Finding the right balance means incorporating intentional stimuli that bring joy and engagement without overwhelming your brain. A small shelf with a favorite book, calming music, or a fidget tool can help make the space feel welcoming without becoming a source of distraction.

Using technology wisely can also make a difference. Instead of letting screens become a source of endless distraction, use tools that enhance focus and structure. A Pomodoro timer can help create natural work-rest cycles, while curated playlists of low-stimulation background music can keep you engaged without pulling your attention away from the task at hand.

Monitoring your energy levels is key to making The Shelter work long-term. Some days, you might feel mentally wired and overstimulated, while other days, you might struggle with brain fog and low motivation. Paying attention to these shifts can help you adjust your environment and routines accordingly. If you're feeling overwhelmed, the Shelter can become a space to reset—taking a few moments to breathe deeply, step away from screens, or engage in a creative hobby that helps you feel more grounded. If you're feeling sluggish, using movement—even standing up, stretching, or changing your workspace—can help signal your brain that it's time to shift gears.

At its core, The Shelter isn't just a space—it's a system of support that helps you work with your ADHD brain instead of against it. It provides stability in the midst of chaos, giving you a structured way to stay focused, recharge, and celebrate progress. You create a foundation for long-term success, sustainability, and balance by intentionally designing an environment that meets your brain's needs.

The Shelter is More than Just a Physical Space; It's a Place to Balance the Storm

Your shelter is a tool to help you manage the natural ebb and flow of dopamine in your ADHD brain. By providing a safe haven where stimulation is balanced and intentional, the Shelter allows you to regain focus, recover from burnout, and move through life with greater clarity and resilience.

Understanding how dopamine works in your brain is empowering. It's not about fixing or changing who you are—it's about working with your brain's natural rhythms to create an environment where you can thrive. Your Shelter is that environment, offering calm amidst the storm and a space where your unique strengths can shine.

Stress Response and Cortisol in ADHD

ADHD is also associated with a heightened stress response. Studies have shown that individuals with ADHD may produce higher levels of cortisol (the stress hormone) in reaction to challenging or emotionally charged situations. This hyper-reactive stress response can make individuals feel as though they are "always on alert," leading to emotional fatigue and, over time, burnout. Your Shelter can be a safe, peaceful environment that reduces the frequency and intensity of these stress responses. In a personal "shelter," individuals with ADHD can decompress, allowing cortisol levels to drop and providing the nervous system with an opportunity to recalibrate. Without regular moments of shelter, chronic stress can exacerbate ADHD symptoms and impact overall health.

Sensory Processing Sensitivity and ADHD

Many people with ADHD are more sensitive to sensory stimuli—sounds, lights, textures, and even the emotional atmosphere of a room can feel more intense. This sensitivity is due, in part, to differences in the brain's sensory processing centers, which may respond to external stimuli with heightened alertness or exaggerated reactions. This hyper-responsiveness can lead to sensory overload, especially in noisy, chaotic, or crowded environments, which can contribute to stress and anxiety.

What can a shelter do for you? A personal shelter provides a controlled sensory environment where individuals can adjust stimuli to comfortable levels, reducing the risk of sensory overload. This can be as simple as having a quiet room with dim lighting, soft textures, and minimal distractions. By intentionally creating a space that minimizes sensory triggers, individuals with ADHD can better manage their sensory input, which in turn helps regulate their emotional responses.

The ADHD Brain's Need for Restorative Downtime

The ADHD brain typically has much less energy than a neurotypical brain. Although many individuals with ADHD are recognized for their high-energy bursts and spontaneous productivity, their brains and bodies also strongly require restorative downtime. Unlike neurotypical individuals, who are often able to maintain attention and productivity more consistently, those with ADHD frequently encounter cyclical energy patterns. The brain can transition from intense focus to mental fatigue, especially after extended periods of stimulation or multitasking. Having a space to retreat to allows for restorative breaks that align with the natural fluctuations of the ADHD brain. Downtime in a comfortable, low-stimulation environment allows the brain to recharge, making it easier to sustain focus and productivity when returning to tasks.

Emotional Regulation Challenges and the Role of Safe Spaces

Emotional regulation is often a challenge for those with ADHD due to differences in the prefrontal cortex, the area of the brain involved in impulse control and emotional processing. This can result in heightened emotional responses, difficulty managing stress, and increased vulnerability to criticism. Without proper support, individuals with ADHD may experience frequent emotional exhaustion or cycles of self-criticism that affect self-esteem. This is where a personal "shelter" becomes a critical space for processing emotions without judgment or interruption. Whether it's a physical room where they can decompress or a routine of self-reflection and self-compassion, this shelter allows individuals to release pent-up emotions and engage in practices that reinforce positive self-image and emotional resilience.

ADHD, Sleep Patterns, and the Importance of Calm Environments

It is critically important to have a good night's sleep. For many, including myself, a good night's sleep is non-negotiable if I want to accomplish anything. Sleep disturbances are common among individuals with ADHD, often due to irregular circadian rhythms and difficulties in "shutting off" an active mind. Many people with ADHD report struggling to fall asleep or waking up frequently throughout the night, leading to chronic sleep deprivation, which can worsen ADHD symptoms. When sleep is disrupted, cognitive functions like memory, focus, and emotional regulation suffer. The Role of the Shelter should ideally include practices or spaces promoting relaxation and good sleep hygiene. This might involve setting up a bedtime routine in a quiet, darkened room or engaging in calming pre-sleep activities like reading a book, deep breathing, or gentle stretching. A well-designed shelter supports restful sleep, helping mitigate some of the cognitive and emotional challenges of sleep deprivation.

Building Long-Term Resilience through Physiological Balance

Lastly, by understanding how ADHD affects the body and mind on a physiological level, individuals can develop a comprehensive approach to managing their symptoms. The shelter can serve as a foundation for building resilience and enhancing overall well-being. Practicing regular stress-relief techniques, engaging in physical activities that boost dopamine (such as exercise or hobbies), and learning to tune in to one's physiological needs are all part of maintaining this "shelter." The Role of Shelter is to create routines supporting the ADHD brain's physiological needs. Regular exercise, balanced nutrition, hydration, and sleep provide a base layer of resilience. These healthy habits, supported by a nurturing environment, help sustain cognitive function and emotional stability over time.

The Blueprints of Your Shelter

Let's build your shelter and put it into practice. Here are some Ideas that will help you begin your design.

Design a Calming Physical Space: Reduce clutter, incorporate soft lighting, and add sensory-friendly elements, like textured blankets, soothing scents, or noise-canceling options.

Establish a Routine for Downtime: Integrate restorative activities, such as mindful breathing, meditation, or quiet hobbies, into daily life to allow for mental relaxation.

Create a Sensory Toolkit: Collect items that provide comfort, such as earplugs for noise, sunglasses for light sensitivity, or fidget tools for tactile engagement.

Build a Support Network: Connect with friends, family, or support groups that offer understanding, encouragement, and validation, acting as an emotional "shelter."

Focus on Health Basics: Prioritize sleep, nutrition, and exercise to create a strong physical foundation. This physiological balance is crucial for sustaining resilience and effectively managing ADHD symptoms.

Develop Emotional Resilience Practices: For individuals with ADHD, emotions can often feel intense, and moments of frustration or self-doubt can be frequent. To cultivate resilience, readers can create personal rituals that offer emotional shelter. For example:

Daily Reflection Journals: Set aside a few minutes each day to write down feelings, positive accomplishments, or areas of gratitude. This provides a safe emotional outlet and helps individuals track patterns, celebrating small wins along the way.

Positive Affirmations and Self-Compassion Exercises: Practicing affirmations or using self-compassion prompts like, "I am learning and growing" or "It's okay to take a break" can help counter self-critical thoughts that may arise from living with ADHD.

Design a Mindfulness Practice for Daily Shelter Moments: Since the ADHD brain can feel constantly "on," finding moments of calm helps slow down this rapid pace. Introduce the concept of "shelter moments":

Breathing Exercises: Techniques like deep belly breathing or the 4-7-8 method help ground and calm the mind. These can be practiced for five minutes during work breaks or before starting a challenging task.

Mindful Walks or Grounding Activities: Stepping outside for a few minutes to engage the senses with nature or just taking a mindful walk can provide mental space and reduce feelings of overwhelm.

Visualization Practices: Visualizing a "shelter" as a mental escape—a cozy cabin, a tranquil beach, or any peaceful place that brings calm—can offer mental refuge during stressful moments. This mental shelter becomes a portable sanctuary that individuals can access anytime.

Incorporate Technology Mindfully: Technology can be a double-edged sword for those with ADHD, as it provides both distraction and support. Creating a shelter includes mindful use of tech:

Use Apps for Focus and Relaxation: Apps like Calm or Headspace can help build mindfulness habits, while focus apps like Forest or Pomodoro timers aid in managing work sessions effectively.

Set Boundaries with Notifications: Turning off non-essential notifications, especially during focus time, creates a quieter environment and helps avoid sensory overload.

Curate Online Spaces: Encourage readers to develop a "digital shelter"—spaces online that foster positivity and community rather than overstimulation. This might mean connecting with ADHD support groups or following uplifting social media accounts.

Connect with ADHD-Friendly Communities: Having a social "shelter" is equally important, where individuals can seek encouragement, share challenges, and find camaraderie with others who understand ADHD firsthand. —Some options include:

Support Groups: Many communities offer local ADHD support groups where individuals can meet and share experiences in a safe, judgment-free environment. Online Forums and Communities: Social media groups or virtual meet-ups provide a broader network of people who can offer advice, empathy, and support.

Therapy and Coaching: Partnering with a therapist or ADHD coach familiar with the condition can help provide professional guidance, structure, and motivation to build a personalized shelter strategy.

Set Boundaries to Protect Your Shelter: ADHD often involves a heightened sensitivity to external demands, social pressures, and the tendency to take on too much, leading to overwhelm. Learning to set clear boundaries is essential:

Learn to Say No Without Guilt: Practice politely declining invitations or tasks that seem too demanding, using phrases like "I can't commit right now" or "I'd love to, but my schedule is full."

Limit Time with Negative Influences: Minimizing interactions with people or environments that trigger stress or self-doubt helps reinforce a safe mental space.

Designate "Off Time" for Recovery: Allow time each day or week without obligations or social commitments. This designated downtime acts as a "closed shelter" where you can recharge without external demands.

Physical Activity as a Source of Shelter and Resilience: Physical activity isn't just for physical health—it has direct benefits for ADHD, especially when it comes to dopamine production, mood regulation, and mental clarity.

Incorporate Movement into Daily Life: Whether it's a 10-minute morning stretch, a quick walk after lunch, or a favorite sport, regular movement routines act as shelter moments, helping the brain relax and reset.

Explore Low-Stimulation Activities for Relaxation: For individuals with ADHD who find traditional exercise overwhelming, recommend calming activities like yoga, tai chi, or gentle swimming. These forms of movement are especially useful for reducing stress without overstimulating the senses.

These are all the tools and components used to harness the various elements of the storm. Together, they form the building blocks of your shelter.

Connecting Your Shelter to Your Physiological Needs

The shelter isn't only about self-care and environmental design; it teaches that understanding ADHD's physiological traits can help construct the most supportive shelter possible.

We know that recharging through physiological awareness creates a shelter that meets ADHD's unique physiological needs and allows individuals to tap into the body's natural cycles of energy and rest. Unlike neurotypical minds, ADHD often involves shifting energy and focus levels, which can fluctuate dramatically throughout the day or week. Embracing these cycles, rather than fighting them, is key. By designing a shelter that promotes both mental rest and physical self-care, you learn to work with, rather than against, your ADHD. You create a space where the demands of life are tempered by a consistent, nurturing environment that respects your body's cues.

Finally, the shelter reinforces emotional resilience by becoming a reliable space where you can process feelings, reflect, and refocus. By equipping you with tools like mindfulness, journaling, and self-compassion, the shelter becomes a trusted place to recalibrate. These tools ensure that even in moments of vulnerability or burnout, there is a protected space where you can rebuild your emotional reserves.

Strengthening the Shelter For Stability and Growth

The shelter is more than a temporary refuge; it's a foundation that you can rely on throughout your life. Here, we explore how to make your shelter a permanent, evolving part of daily life as a way to manage challenges and as a proactive approach to well-being, growth, and self-empowerment.

As you grow and change, so do your needs and preferences for shelter. The ADHD journey is not static; it can evolve as circumstances shift— new jobs, relationships, and stages of life all present unique challenges and opportunities. It is crucial to periodically reassess your shelter to ensure it remains effective and aligns with your current reality. Check in every few months to evaluate your shelter setup, considering whether your routines, self-care practices, and physical environments still meet your needs. You can ask questions like, "Is my space cluttered or peaceful? Do I have regular downtime? Is my support network still active and reliable?" Transitions are a part of life. Examine your shelter's foundations during major transitions (such as moving, starting a new job, or entering a new relationship) to ensure it supports you through change. For instance, you might adjust a work-from-home setup to reduce distractions or integrate new friends into your social "shelter" if you are relocating.

Reinforcing the Shelter Through Self-Awareness and Self-Compassion

Building a solid shelter requires an ongoing practice of self-awareness. By continually observing how ADHD impacts your daily life, you can better understand your patterns, triggers, and strengths. Self-compassion becomes equally vital in this journey, allowing you to navigate challenges without self-criticism.

Self-Reflection: Journaling can be an effective self-reflection tool. It helps people track what works, what doesn't, and how their ADHD symptoms evolve. For instance, you might note days when you felt especially overwhelmed and what helped, or reflect on the supportive routines you managed to sustain.

Practicing Self-Forgiveness: For many with ADHD, self-criticism is an ongoing struggle. It's important to practice forgiving yourself for moments when you feel you've "failed" or haven't met certain expectations. Self-compassion reminds you that ADHD often means adjusting expectations and giving yourself the grace to grow at your own pace.

Using Mindful Boundaries to Protect and Preserve the Shelter

Boundaries are critical to maintaining a peaceful and restorative shelter. Without boundaries, the shelter can be eroded by others' demands, over-stimulation, or the internal pressures individuals with ADHD often face. Here are specific techniques for setting and enforcing boundaries.

Personal Boundaries for Rest and Recharge: Set specific hours for personal downtime, during which external demands are minimized. For example, you could designate a "quiet hour" each night to wind down without screens or interactions, creating space for mental recovery.

Workplace Boundaries for Focus and Balance: In the workplace, setting boundaries might mean controlling one's schedule, blocking out focus periods, or setting expectations with colleagues. Practicing saying "no" to additional tasks can help protect one's energy and allow for better productivity within the confines of set work hours.

Digital Boundaries to Reduce Overwhelm: Digital notifications, social media, and constant connectivity can erode the shelter's effectiveness. To mitigate possible overwhelm, try limiting screen time, using "do not disturb" features, or regularly trying digital detoxes. This will allow the shelter to remain a space of mental quiet.

Establishing Rituals that Anchor the Shelter in Daily Life

Rituals bring familiarity, structure, and comfort, acting as anchors that hold the shelter steady even when life's storms rage. For people with ADHD who may struggle with consistency, integrating small, meaningful rituals can provide grounding and a sense of security.

Morning and Evening Routines: Morning rituals set a positive tone, while evening rituals signal winding down. For example, a short meditation, writing a to-do list, or a Hot cup of Herbal tea each evening can help you relax in the shelter's safety before bed.

Weekly Reset Rituals: A weekly "reset" where you can organize your space, declutter, and prepare for the week ahead. This helps reinforce your shelter's physical and mental stability, keeping it a clean, organized space that feels inviting.

Reflection Rituals: Creating a habit of regular self-reflection—whether it's a weekly journaling session or a monthly personal check-in—helps maintain alignment with personal goals and reaffirms the shelter's role as a place of growth and support.

Building Resilience with Support Systems and Connections

A shelter is strongest when reinforced by supportive relationships. Having people who understand ADHD and can offer empathy and encouragement is like adding extra beams to the shelter's structure, making it more resilient. Cultivating connections that uplift and validate the ADHD experience can be especially beneficial. Some of these connections may include the following:

Friends and Family as Allies: Building a support system with friends or family who respect boundaries, offer a listening ear, and are sensitive to ADHD's unique challenges can make a significant difference. This might include asking close friends to check in during stressful times or sharing victories and challenges with loved ones.

Professional Support: Therapists, ADHD coaches, or counselors offer expert guidance and are an invaluable part of a supportive shelter. Regular therapy or coaching sessions provide structured time for self-reflection, problem-solving, and accountability.

Community Engagement: Participating in ADHD support groups or communities allows you to connect with others who understand your experiences on a deeper level. These communities offer insights, shared strategies, and mutual encouragement, reducing the isolation that ADHD can sometimes cause.

Maintaining Balance Through Adaptable Self-Care

Flexibility is key in ADHD management. Because ADHD symptoms and needs can change daily or weekly, a rigid self-care routine may feel unrealistic. Work to develop adaptable self-care practices that you can adjust according to your energy, mood, and focus levels.

Flexible Self-Care Plans: Rather than a strict routine, suggest having a menu of self-care options that you can choose from based on how you feel each day. These options might include taking a walk, journaling, engaging in creative hobbies, or practicing mindfulness.

Low-Effort Self-Care for Tough Days: On particularly challenging days, simple, comforting activities that don't require much effort (like drinking a favorite beverage, listening to relaxing music, or doing a brief breathing exercise) serve as gentle shelter reinforcements.

Checking in with Physical Needs: Since physical well-being impacts mental health, you should include basic care practices (hydration, nutrition, movement, and sleep) in your shelter routine. Addressing these foundational needs supports the ADHD brain's resilience and strengthens the shelter's overall stability.

We tie together the shelter's purpose as a place of ongoing peace and growth amid life's storms. It's essential to remember that the shelter doesn't eliminate the challenges of ADHD or shield individuals from every external stressor, but it provides a safe space to regroup, process, and prepare for each new day. Building and maintaining your shelter will take time and adjustments. The shelter doesn't need to be perfect; it simply needs to feel safe and supportive. You should approach this space with flexibility and compassion, understanding that it will evolve with your needs.

Practicing Gratitude for Small Wins: Regularly expressing gratitude for the progress made, even small steps, can reinforce the sense of security within the shelter. Celebrate victories like establishing a successful routine, saying no to something overwhelming, or finding a comforting self-care ritual.

Embracing the Shelter as a Foundation for Future Growth: The shelter is not just a place of refuge; it's a base for thriving, where you can build the resilience and confidence needed to navigate the world. By creating a safe, nurturing space within and around yourself, you will be equipped to face both daily challenges and larger life transitions with greater stability and strength.

The Shelter creates a comprehensive approach to building, maintaining, and evolving a safe space for your life with ADHD. The shelter serves as both a physical and emotional sanctuary where you can recharge, adapt, and fortify yourself against external and internal stressors.

In conclusion, I leave you with a sense of hope and empowerment, reminding you that while life with ADHD may feel like a storm, you possess the tools to create a place of calm, self-acceptance, and resilience. Connecting the Shelter to ADHD's Physiological Needs

Let's talk about something close to my heart. You've been navigating life with ADHD, and it's not easy, is it? It's like a rollercoaster with its ups and downs, moments of incredible energy and creativity, followed by stretches where even getting out of bed feels like climbing a mountain. That's where this concept of *The Shelter* comes in. It's not just a nice idea—it's something deeply tied to how your brain works, and it's a way to support yourself, physically and emotionally, in the best way possible. So, let's dive in together as we explore this crucial element.

Recharging Through Physiological Awareness

Let me tell you something important: Your ADHD brain has its rhythm. It's not "wrong" or "broken"; it's just different. Think of it as a tide—sometimes it rushes in with energy, focus, and ideas, and other times it ebbs, leaving you feeling drained. And that's okay. Fighting against these natural rhythms will only leave you frustrated and exhausted. What you need is a space—a shelter—that lets you work with those rhythms instead of against them.

I'll give you an example. My friend Alex has ADHD, and he used to get so frustrated with himself for not being able to focus in the afternoons. He'd beat himself up, thinking he was lazy or unmotivated. But when he started to track his energy patterns, he realized that his focus was sharpest in the mornings and late evenings. So, he created a "shelter routine" that respected that: mornings were for his hardest tasks, afternoons were for recharging in a quiet, clutter-free space, and evenings were for creativity. It wasn't about fixing himself; it was about working with himself. That shift made all the difference.

Your shelter can do the same for you. It's not just a physical space; it's a system that respects your body's cues, giving you the rest you need when you're low on energy and the structure you crave when you're ready to tackle the world.

Building Long-Term Emotional Resilience

Here's the thing about life with ADHD: it's intense. Your emotions can feel like tidal waves—highs that make you feel unstoppable and lows that leave you questioning everything. And let me tell you, that's not a flaw. It's just part of how you're wired. But to ride those waves without being swept away, you need a safe space where you can process, reflect, and recharge.

Think of it like this: your shelter is your emotional anchor. It's where you can journal about your day, practice mindfulness, or simply sit with your thoughts without judgment. I'll share another story. My cousin Rachel has ADHD, and she used to avoid her feelings because they felt too over-whelming. But when she started keeping a journal, her shelter became a space where she could let it all out—her fears, her frustrations, her dreams. Over time, she realized that naming her emotions didn't make them scarier; it made them manageable. Your shelter can do that for you —it's your place to breathe, recalibrate, and remind yourself that you've got this!

Strengthening the Shelter: Long-Term Strategies for Stability and Growth

Your shelter isn't a one-and-done kind of thing. It's something you build, maintain, and adapt as your needs change. Life is messy, unpredictable, and full of curveballs, and that's especially true when you're managing ADHD. But your shelter can evolve with you, becoming a constant source of support.

As you grow and change, so do your shelter needs and preferences. The ADHD journey is not static; it can evolve as circumstances shift. New jobs, relationships, and stages of life all bring unique challenges and opportunities. Importantly, you need to periodically reassess your shelter to help keep it effective and aligned with your current reality.

Evaluate your shelter setup every few months to determine if your routines, self-care practices, and physical environment still meet your needs. You can ask questions like, "Is my space cluttered or peaceful? Do I have regular downtime? Is my support network still active and reliable?"

During major transitions (moving, starting a new job, or entering a new relationship), you can look at your shelter's foundations to ensure it supports you through change. For instance, adjusting a work-from-home setup to reduce distractions or integrating new friends into your social "shelter" if relocating.

Making it enduring and central to daily life

Living with ADHD means acknowledging that the challenges it brings are unlikely to disappear entirely, but they can be managed, harnessed, and even appreciated. The shelter provides a space where these challenges are met with compassion and understanding rather than frustration. By accepting ADHD as a part of life rather than something to "fix," you allow yourself the grace to make mistakes, take breaks, and find strategies that align with your unique needs.

Recognize that ADHD brings unique perspectives and strengths, such as creativity, resilience, and curiosity, alongside its challenges. These strengths can be nurtured and celebrated within the shelter, helping you build self-confidence and embrace your authentic self.

The shelter isn't static; it can expand, evolve, and adapt alongside the individual. Over time, you may find new tools, relationships, and routines that enhance your shelter, making it a dynamic environment that reflects your growth.

You should periodically reflect on how the shelter is serving you. This can involve asking questions like, "What aspects of my shelter feel supportive?" or "Where could I make adjustments to better meet my current needs?" Regular reflection helps ensure that the shelter continues to feel relevant and empowering. The shelter supports a vision of balance—a life where you can manage your symptoms while pursuing fulfillment, connection, and peace. Grounding yourself in routines, relationships, and environments that support you. You build a life that is both protected from being overwhelmed and open to joy and growth.

Set personal intentions for your shelter and your life with ADHD. These intentions might focus on balance, resilience, self-compassion, or even specific goals like deepening relationships or advancing professionally.

Setting intentions creates a vision that brings purpose and motivation to the journey ahead.

Ultimately, "The Shelter" reminds us that true empowerment comes from within. You can find resilience and peace by accepting yourself fully and creating a supportive environment. The shelter encourages you to build and serves as a testament to the strength that comes from embracing one's journey, including all the unique facets of living with ADHD.

Trust the Process. The journey of managing ADHD and building a supportive shelter isn't always linear. Some days may feel challenging, but the shelter becomes dependable with consistent care, self-compassion, and adaptation. You are reminded to trust your journey and believe in your resilience, knowing that you have created a space of safety and strength within yourself. Ideally, it would be appropriate to close with a series of prompts or a reflection exercise, guiding you to envision your own shelter and explore what you want it to represent.

Designing Your Shelter

Take a few moments to envision your shelter. This is your personal, mental, and physical space, providing calm, comfort, and strength. Use the following prompts to guide your thoughts:

Describe Your Ideal Physical Shelter: Imagine a space where you feel at peace. What does it look like? Is it a cozy room, an outdoor retreat, or a quiet corner? List the sensory elements that make this space comforting—sounds, scents, colors, textures.

Identify Three Emotional Needs Your Shelter Meets: What emotional needs do you want your shelter to fulfill? This could be relaxation, encouragement, connection, or protection from stress. How can you build these qualities into your daily routines or environment?

List People Who Contribute to Your Social Shelter: Think of the supportive people in your life who offer understanding, encouragement, and respect for your boundaries. How can you strengthen these relationships and invite them into your shelter?

Set One Intention for Your Shelter: Choose a guiding intention for your shelter. This could be a word like "calm," "growth," or "balance," or a phrase like "I am safe here" or "I am enough." Write this intention down somewhere visible to remind you of your shelter's purpose.

Make a Plan to Revisit and Reinforce Your Shelter: Choose one way to reinforce your shelter in the next month, such as reorganizing a physical space, scheduling time for self-care, or reflecting on your support system. Revisit this plan periodically to keep your shelter strong and adaptable.

Using the reflection exercises will allow you to bring your shelter to life personally and practically. They will help you visualize a place you can return to whenever life feels overwhelming. Thus, this chapter becomes not just a concept but a tangible, empowering space you carry into all aspects of your life.

Embrace the Shelter as a Lasting Resource.

Your journey of living with ADHD and the concept of "The Shelter" serves as a foundation to which you can return, no matter what challenges you face. It represents more than a temporary respite—it is a lifelong resource, something you can continually build, adjust, and reinforce to maintain resilience and peace.

As you conclude this chapter, you are encouraged to view the shelter as an evolving part of your life, a resource that grows with you and provides continuity through various life stages. Whether navigating new jobs, relationships, or personal challenges, this shelter will remain a stable base where you can reconnect with your values, recharge, and find strength.

There are long-term benefits to maintaining the Shelter. By committing to the practices and mindsets outlined in this chapter, you create a powerful, sustainable tool for managing ADHD.

You will gain a greater understanding of a well-maintained shelter, one that fosters self-compassion and teaches you to respond to your ADHD challenges with kindness rather than frustration. As you develop a greater understanding of your unique needs, you will become more adept at handling setbacks and celebrating progress.

Through consistent shelter practices, you build emotional resilience. Having a safe space to process emotions reduces feelings of overwhelm and improves one's ability to face life's ups and downs. The shelter becomes a place to decompress, recalibrate, and gather strength for each new day.

Enhanced Focus and Productivity: With a designated space to recharge, you can approach tasks with renewed energy and focus. The shelter helps manage sensory and emotional overload, enabling you to engage more effectively with your work, relationships, and personal goals.

A Stronger Sense of Purpose and Direction: The shelter isn't just a space for rest—it's a place where you can clarify your goals, values, and intentions. By regularly reflecting on what matters to you, you develop a stronger sense of purpose, allowing you to live in alignment with your values.

Advocate for Your Needs: A clear understanding of what makes a safe, nurturing environment allows you to advocate for yourself in other areas of life. Whether in the workplace, social settings, or relationships, you can express your needs with confidence, building environments that respect and support your unique neurodivergence.

The Shelter is a Symbol of Inner Strength

Throughout these pages, I hope you will see the shelter as a symbol of your inner strength. It's not just a place but a reflection of your resilience, adaptability, and commitment to self-care. The shelter embodies your journey toward self-acceptance, showing that you have the power to create safety, calm, and support from within, regardless of life's external storms.

To bring a sense of closure and continuity, I would like to conclude with a final exercise, inviting you to reflect on your journey with ADHD and how you plan to continue building your shelter.

"The Shelter" closes the loop on the storm metaphor by offering a space to recharge and sustainably protect your well-being. It balances the chaos of ADHD with stability and tranquility, creating an emotional and physical safe haven that empowers you to face life with greater resilience. However, remember that your shelter is always evolving. Therefore, it's essential to adapt strategies to strengthen it.

The Journey Ahead

Consider the following to help you envision how you would like to continue nurturing your shelter and utilizing it as a resource in the future.

Reflect on Your Growth: Consider how your understanding of ADHD and yourself has evolved throughout this book. Write down three insights or realizations that have been most impactful for you. Reflect on how these insights have influenced your sense of self and your approach to life with ADHD.

Define Your Vision for the Future: Imagine your future self living confidently with ADHD. What does that version of you look like? How do you maintain your shelter and stay connected to your values? Describe the qualities, habits, and relationships you hope to cultivate as you continue on this journey.

Set a Shelter-Related Goal: Choose one actionable goal related to maintaining your shelter. It could be as simple as dedicating time for self-reflection each week or as specific as organizing a physical space that brings you peace. Write down this goal and the steps you plan to take to achieve it.

Identify a "Storm" and Plan for Shelter: Think of a challenge you're currently facing or expect to face soon. How can you use your shelter practices to prepare for or navigate this storm? Write down the tools, strategies, or support systems you'll rely on to help you through it.

Remind yourself

You've learned how to build your shelter and cultivate a safe space to manage and harness the storm. However, life will throw curveballs at you, so it's important to frequently remind yourself of the power you possess by creating a reminder of the inner strength you've developed. This could be a phrase, image, or item symbolizing your resilience and growth. Keep it somewhere visible in your shelter to remind you that, even amidst the storm, you have the power to find calm and clarity. You are in control, and you get to decide whether ADHD is your greatest strength or your biggest weakness. Follow what you have learned; it will undoubtedly become your greatest strength. You've got this!

"Each element of the storm carries both challenge and potential. With the right tools, you can embrace the Storm as a source of energy that drives you forward."

CHAPTER 9

The Path Forward

Living with ADHD isn't about "fixing" yourself—it's about understanding who you are, adapting to your needs, and learning how to thrive. Think about it this way: every storm you've faced—whether it's the whirlwind of distractions, the lightning of intense emotions, or the fog of uncertainty—has taught you something valuable. Each chapter in this journey has been about turning those challenges into opportunities for growth, resilience, and self-discovery.

And now, as we stand at this point together, I want you to remember this: You are not defined by ADHD. You are defined by your courage to face the storms, your creativity in navigating them, and your resilience in coming out stronger on the other side. The Shelter you've built is a reflection of that strength—a place where you can rest, recharge, and remind yourself that you are capable of amazing things.

Your Shelter isn't just a metaphor. It's a practical resource. It's the anchor that keeps you steady when the winds of distraction or emotions threaten to pull you off course. It's also your launchpad—a place to dream, create, and build the life you deserve. And here's the beautiful part: this Shelter grows with you. It changes as you do, evolving through every season of your life to meet your needs. Let's explore how you can continue to build on this foundation and what it means for your future.

Celebrate Your Journey Toward Self-Acceptance

I know it hasn't been easy. Living with ADHD can feel like carrying an invisible burden that others don't always understand. But look at everything you've accomplished so far. You've taken the time to learn about yourself, to reflect, and to build a supportive space where you can thrive. That's huge.

Think about a moment recently when you felt truly proud of yourself. Maybe it was completing a task you'd been procrastinating on, setting a boundary, or simply showing yourself some compassion on a tough day. Those moments matter. They're the bricks that build your Shelter and the proof that you're stronger and more capable than you sometimes realize.

I used to be my own worst critic. No matter how much I accomplished, it never felt like enough. I'd finish a project, cross tasks off my list, and even manage to stay on top of things for a while—but instead of feeling accomplished, all I could see were the things I hadn't done: the unfinished projects, the forgotten emails, the moments when I got distracted and felt like I was wasting time. It was as if my brain had a built-in filter that only allowed me to focus on what I hadn't done, completely overlooking everything I had.

Then, one day, I decided to try something different. Instead of mentally beating myself up at the end of the day, I started writing down one small win before bed. Just one, even if it felt insignificant. Some days, it was simple: "I answered that email I've been putting off." Other days, it was more personal, like "I stopped myself from spiraling into negative self-talk." And you know what? Over time, those "small" wins didn't feel so small anymore. I began to realize how much I was truly showing up for myself, pushing through challenges and making progress, even when it didn't feel that way.

That shift changed everything for me. I stopped measuring success by impossible, all-or-nothing standards and started celebrating the journey instead of just the destination. And now, I want to say this to you as clearly as I can: Celebrate yourself. Celebrate every single step forward, no matter how small it feels, because those steps add up. They shape the bigger picture of who you're becoming. They serve as proof that you're moving forward, learning, growing, and showing up for yourself even on the hard days.

So give yourself credit. Recognize the effort, not just the outcome. Every step—every win, every moment of progress—is worth celebrating—and so are you.

A Catalyst for Thriving, Not Just Surviving

Here's something I want you to know: you weren't put on this earth just to endure the storms of ADHD. You're meant to thrive. The shelter you've created isn't merely a place to withstand the chaos—it's a foundation for something greater. It's where you can transform your unique strengths, passions, and dreams into reality.

For so long, people with ADHD have been told what they "can't" do. But let's flip that script. Your ADHD comes with incredible gifts: creativity, resilience, out-of-the-box thinking, and a knack for seeing connections that others miss. The Shelter provides you with the stability to channel those strengths intentionally. When you're grounded, you can:

Pursue Your Passions: With fewer distractions and more emotional balance, you'll have the focus to dive into the things that light you up. My friend Lucas, who loves painting but always felt too scattered to finish anything, started dedicating one hour every evening to his art in his Shelter. Now, his creativity flows like never before.

Build Meaningful Relationships: The Shelter helps you process emotions, set boundaries, and communicate with loved ones in a way that strengthens your connections. My cousin Sarah, for instance, uses her Shelter time to reflect on her relationships and write letters of appreciation to her friends. It's her way of staying connected and showing gratitude.

Turn Challenges Into Growth: ADHD isn't a limitation—it's a lens that lets you approach problems creatively and adapt in ways others might not. Your Shelter is where you remind yourself of that truth.

Redefining What Thriving Means for You

Let's take a moment to envision your future. What does thriving mean to you? Not what others expect, but what *you* truly desire. Success, joy, and fulfillment are personal and distinct for each of us. Your Shelter provides the stability and clarity needed to define those concepts for you and pursue them without fear or feeling overwhelmed.

1.   Pursue Passions and Goals

What excites you? Maybe it's starting a garden, writing a book, or learning a new skill. Your Shelter is the perfect place to take those first steps. My friend Mia always dreamed of baking but felt too scattered to follow recipes. She started setting aside one evening a week in her Shelter for baking, with simple recipes and no pressure. Now, she's turned that passion into a side business selling cookies. "Start small. Block out a little time in your Shelter each week for something you love. Let it grow from there."

2.   Build a Career Aligned with Your Strengths

What are your strengths? Maybe you're great at generating ideas, connecting with people, or working under pressure. Use your Shelter to reflect on how you can align your work with those strengths. For example, my friend Jason, who struggles with structure but thrives in fast-paced environments, found his niche in event planning. His Shelter became the space where he brainstormed ideas and organized his schedule in ways that worked for him.

3.   Foster Joyful Relationships

Relationships are a huge part of thriving. Use your Shelter to nurture the ones that matter most. My neighbor Lauren, who struggles with emotional overwhelm, set up a routine where she takes a few minutes each evening to reflect on her relationships. She writes down one thing she's grateful for about her partner or friends, which helps her stay connected and positive.

Your Platform for Growth

Growth isn't about having everything figured out overnight. It's about building something strong and steady, one step at a time. That's what your Shelter is—it's the foundation that holds you up, the space that helps you thrive in a world that often feels overwhelming. It's where you set inspiring goals, not as rigid demands, but as reminders of the direction you want to go. Whether your goals are big or small, write them down and keep them visible—let them be the signposts that guide you forward, even on the days when motivation feels far away. Make time each week to reflect and adjust. Check in with yourself, celebrate what's working, and give yourself permission to tweak what isn't. Growth isn't about perfection but learning, adjusting, and moving forward with intention. As you work toward your goals, remember that rest is just as important as effort. Thriving isn't about pushing yourself to exhaustion—it's about recognizing that recharging is part of the process and that giving yourself space to breathe is just as valuable as the work itself.

If you've ever asked yourself, *Can I really do this?*, let me be the one to answer: Yes. Absolutely. Without a doubt. And I don't just mean that in some empty, motivational-poster kind of way—I mean it because I've seen what you've already overcome. Thriving with ADHD isn't about getting everything right all the time. It's not about suddenly becoming perfectly organized, never forgetting things, or turning into a nonstop productivity machine. It's about creating a life that actually works for you—one where you feel safe, capable, and in control, even when things don't go perfectly.

You've been building your Shelter all along, even if you didn't realize it. Every habit you've worked on, every time you've asked for help, every boundary you've set, every moment where you stopped and reminded yourself to keep going—those are the bricks that make up your foundation. And when you look back, you'll see that you've already come so much farther than you thought. You've faced storms that might have knocked others down, but you're still here. Still learning. Still growing. That's not small—it's huge. And now, my friend, you are ready to step forward with confidence, knowing you have the tools, the resilience, and the strength to create a life that supports you, not one that fights against you.

So when doubt creeps in, a tough day makes you question everything, or you feel like you're not making progress fast enough, remind yourself of this: You've got this. Not because life will always be easy, but because you are strong, resourceful, and fully capable of navigating whatever comes next. And no matter what, I'll always be here, rooting for you.

Embrace Your Journey

Take a moment to reflect on everything you've learned. What does your Shelter mean to you? How will you use it to support your dreams, your growth, and your well-being? Write it down. Let this be your roadmap for the path ahead.

Remember, you're not alone in this journey. Your Shelter, community, and resilience are here to guide you. Now, step forward with confidence. The storm may rage, but you've got the tools—and the strength—to thrive.

Acknowledgments

Writing *Harnessing the Storm* has been a deeply personal and transformative journey that would not have been possible without the unwavering support, inspiration, and encouragement of so many incredible people.

First and foremost, I want to thank Shanna, my rock and my greatest supporter. Your patience, love, and belief in me have carried me through the most challenging moments of this process. Your encouragement has given me the strength to keep going when the storm felt overwhelming.

To my family, who may not have always understood my path but have shaped the person I've become—thank you. To my father, Rayburn Dale Ashley, and my father-in-law, Wayne Boring, a Vietnam veteran who served with honor, I am grateful for the resilience and integrity you both instilled in me.

A heartfelt thank you to those who have walked this journey with me— friends, mentors, and fellow ADHD warriors—who reminded me that our storms are not meant to be battled alone. Your stories, struggles, and triumphs have fueled my commitment to this mission.

To the ADHD community—the dreamers, creators, innovators, and relentless thinkers who refuse to be defined by limits—you are the reason for this book. Your stories, challenges, and victories continue to inspire me, and I am honored to be part of this journey with you.

A special thank you to Dr. Stephen Faraone and the ADHD Management Project. Dr. Faraone's research, insights, and real-world experiences shared within this project laid the foundation for this book, providing both the science and the lived experience needed to create practical, meaningful strategies. His work, along with the ADHD Evidence Project, has deepened our understanding of dopamine regulation, executive function, and emotional regulation, shaping many of the core concepts explored in these pages.

To the incredible minds behind the research studies on exercise and ADHD, brain function in neurodivergence, and cognitive behavioral therapy, thank you for your contributions to the field. Your work continues to push the boundaries of how we understand and support those with ADHD.

Finally, to my readers, thank you for choosing to embrace your storm. This book is for you, and I hope it empowers you to turn your ADHD into the incredible force it was meant to be.

Let's harness the storm together.

With gratitude,
Sean M. Ashley

.

Join Us on the Journey

The journey of harnessing the storm doesn't end here—it's just beginning. I invite you to become part of our growing community, where you'll find the tools, support, and encouragement to continue thriving with ADHD. My passion around ADHD isn't a selfish Journey. It's one I want to share with everyone. My Heart goes out to anyone whose life has been impacted by ADHD. I am continually developing and expanding our community and resources to give you an experience like no other. You can - Dive into our supplemental self-awareness journal, which is a companion guide for this book, designed to help you apply the strategies from Harnessing the Storm in real life.

- Get inspired by tuning into our blog or podcast—a place where we share insights, stories, and expert advice to keep you motivated.

- Find Your People: Connect with others on a similar journey. Our community is built on encouragement, support, and the shared goal of making life a little bit better each day.

You are not alone in this storm. We're here to help you navigate, grow, and thrive. Join us today—I can't wait to see you there!

www.itswhatmattersmost.com

About The Author

For most of my life, I have worked in a hands-on profession that taught me how to solve problems, create solutions, and adapt to any challenge. But behind the work, I faced a challenge that wasn't as straightforward to fix—living with ADHD. For years, it shaped my experiences in ways I didn't fully understand. It has influenced my successes, struggles, and relationships as a husband and father. The pressure, self-doubt, and misunderstandings took their toll, but through self-discovery, faith, and persistence, I found a path forward. Learning how ADHD impacted my life allowed me to rebuild relationships, develop self-compassion, and create systems that worked for me rather than against me.

Driven by a desire to help others on a similar journey, I founded "What Matters Most," a space dedicated to supporting neurodivergent individuals with practical tools, resources, and encouragement. Through my books, podcast, and products, I share insights gained from real-life experience, offering not just strategies for success but hope and understanding.

When I'm not working on new projects, I find joy in life's simplest yet most meaningful moments—hiking in the forest, reconnecting with God, and reflecting on what truly matters. My journey has been anything but linear, but I believe that with faith, persistence, and a little grace, we can all find a way forward—one step at a time.

www.ingramcontent.com/pod-product-compliance
Lightning Source LLC
Chambersburg PA
CBHW070333130626
46556CB00007B/2840